MARCH

A TALE OF NEGLECT

A STORY BY ONRIE KOMPAN

Printed in South Korea.

Book and logo design by Joel Saavedra.

We are actively seeking to sell publishing rights, foreign and domestic. For distribution inquiries or other business, please contact Onrie Kompan Productions, 1870 Mission Hills Lane, Northbrook, IL 60062.

OLKompan@gmail.com

I dedicate this work to my family and to my children.

This is my grandfather as I knew him.

SPECIAL THANKS TO:

Will Eisner, Jim Salicrup, David Anthony Kraft, The Chicago Association of Russian WWII Veterans, Vladimir and Irina Kompan, Elona and Dmitry Balyasny, Anna Melnik, Sasha Chusmear and the Chusmear Family, The Alimbayev Family, my wife Khalima, and to Marx for sharing his story with me and the world.

CHAPTER 1:
A FAMILY MATTER

Onrie Kompan
WRITER

Nick Bell
ARTIST & COLORIST

Ed Dukeshire
LETTERER

JM DeMatteis
EDITOR

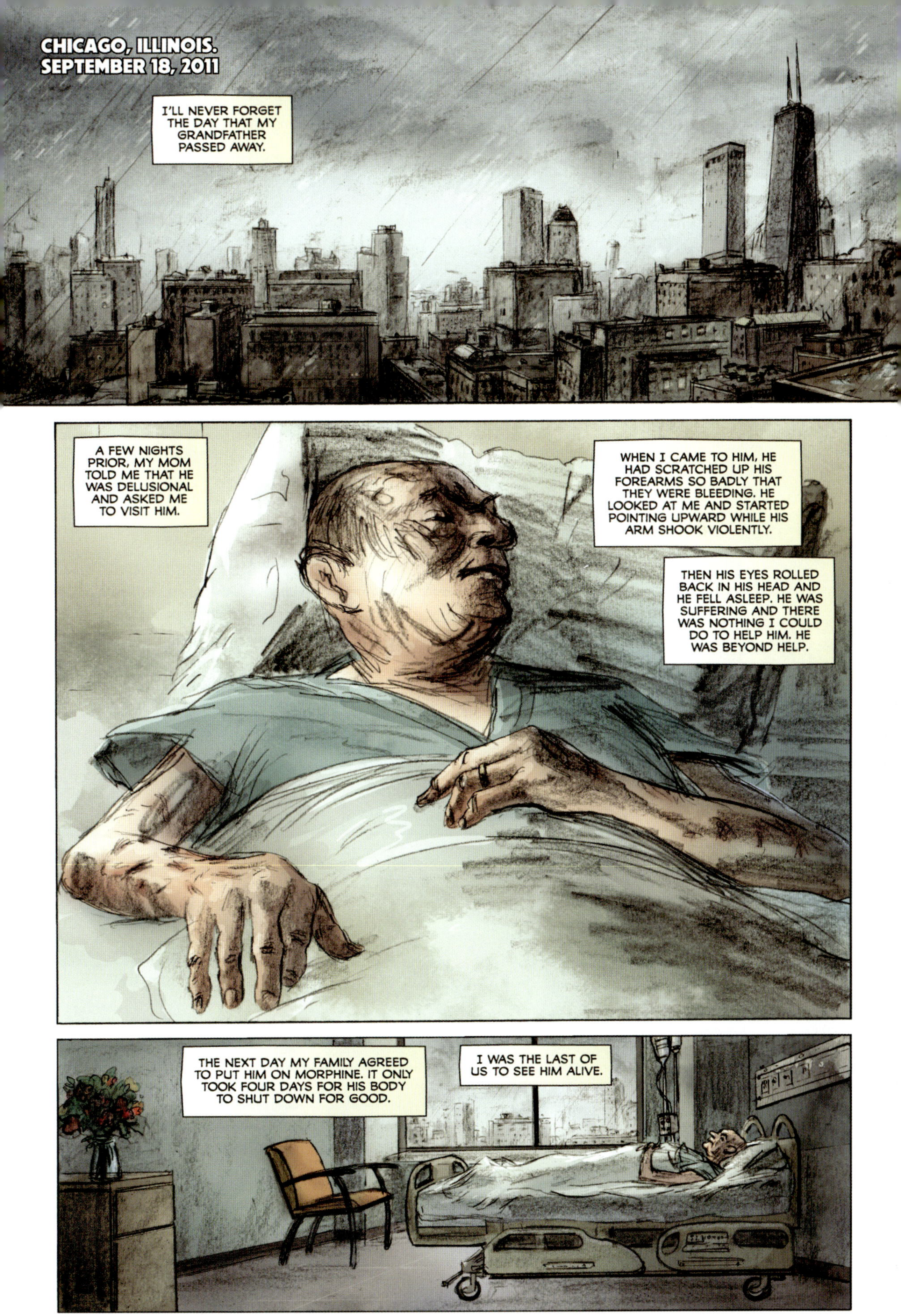

A FEW NIGHTS PRIOR, MY MOM TOLD ME THAT HE WAS DELUSIONAL AND ASKED ME TO VISIT HIM.

WHEN I CAME TO HIM, HE HAD SCRATCHED UP HIS FOREARMS SO BADLY THAT THEY WERE BLEEDING. HE LOOKED AT ME AND STARTED POINTING UPWARD WHILE HIS ARM SHOOK VIOLENTLY.

THEN HIS EYES ROLLED BACK IN HIS HEAD AND HE FELL ASLEEP. HE WAS SUFFERING AND THERE WAS NOTHING I COULD DO TO HELP HIM. HE WAS BEYOND HELP.

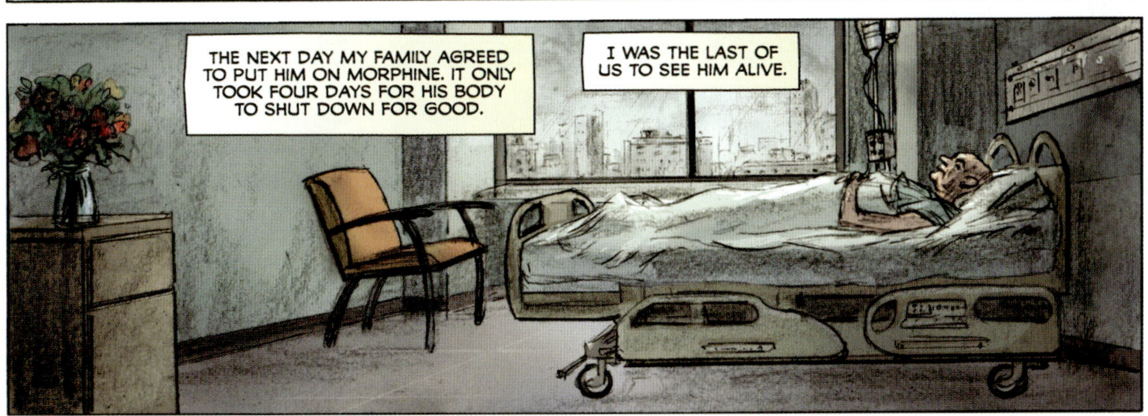

MY GRANDFATHER WAS NO ORDINARY MAN. HE LED AN EXTRAORDINARY LIFE. THEREFORE, I MADE A PLEDGE TO HIM THAT I WOULD TELL HIS STORY.
HE NEVER LIKED TALKING ABOUT HIS PAST MUCH. IT TOOK ME YEARS OF PRYING TO GET WHAT I COULD OUT OF HIM. HIS STORY BEGAN ON A RAINY MORNING IN KHARKOV, UKRAINE ON JULY 16, 1923.

SIR, YOU'RE NOT ALLOWED BACK THERE!
I'M HERE TO SEE MY WIFE! SHE JUST GAVE BIRTH!

DR. MELNIK! PLEASE PARDON ME FOR NOT RECOGNIZING YOU.
IT'S QUITE ALL RIGHT. HOW IS SHE? HOW IS MY ELIZABETH?
SHE HAD A DIFFICULT DELIVERY BUT SHE'S STABLE NOW. I'LL TAKE YOU TO HER.

MY GRANDFATHER KNEW VERY LITTLE ABOUT HIS FATHER, DR. MOSES MELNIK. THEY DIDN'T REALLY SPEND MUCH TIME TOGETHER.
MOSES DIED WHEN MY GRANDFATHER WAS FOURTEEN YEARS OLD, BUT I'LL GET TO THAT LATER.

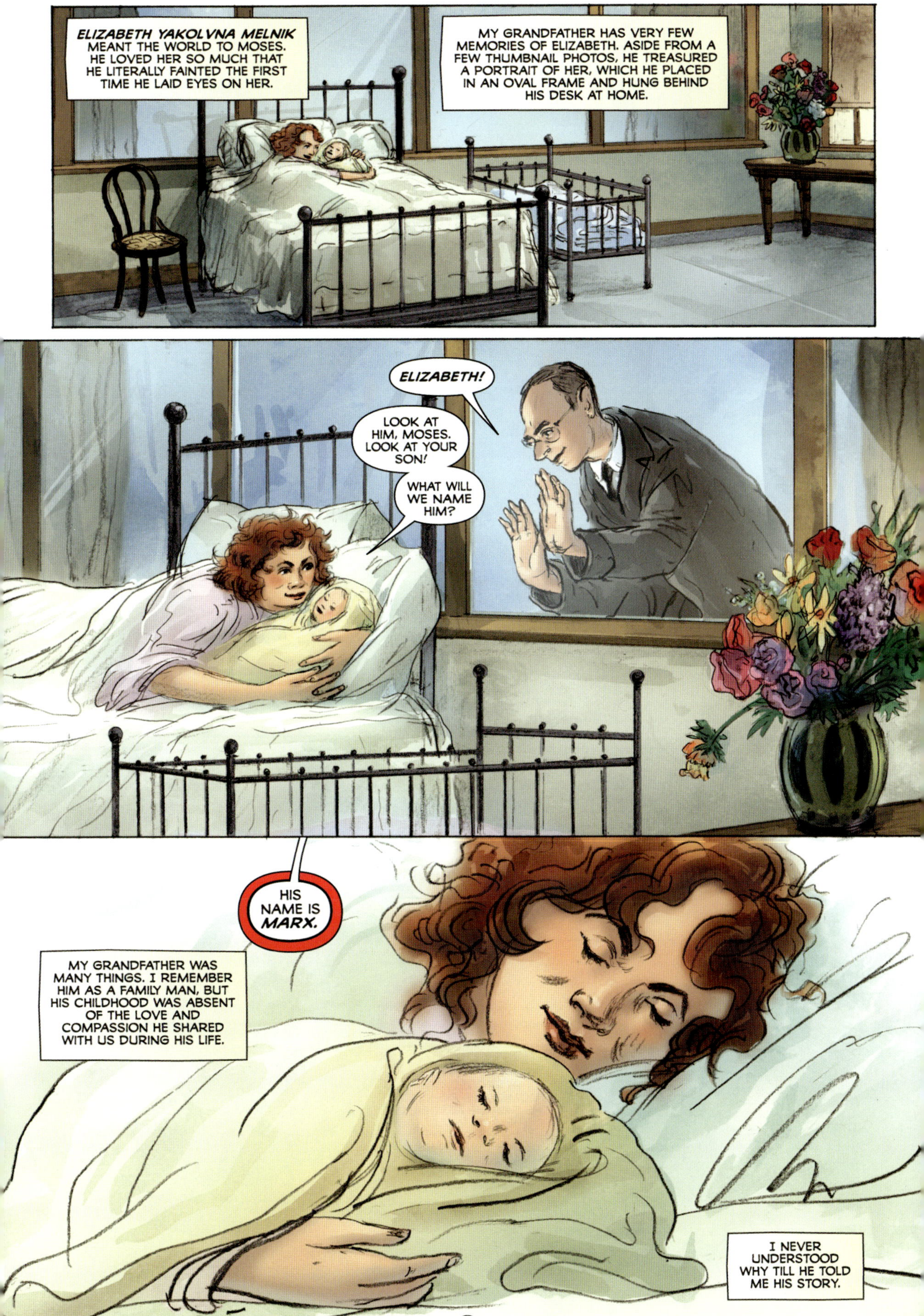

ELIZABETH!

LOOK AT HIM, MOSES. LOOK AT YOUR SON!

WHAT WILL WE NAME HIM?

HIS NAME IS *MARX.*

MY GRANDFATHER WAS MANY THINGS. I REMEMBER HIM AS A FAMILY MAN, BUT HIS CHILDHOOD WAS ABSENT OF THE LOVE AND COMPASSION HE SHARED WITH US DURING HIS LIFE.

I NEVER UNDERSTOOD WHY TILL HE TOLD ME HIS STORY.

KHARKOV, UKRAINE 1926.

...I'VE ACCEPTED THE JOB OFFER AT PASTEUR INSTITUTE.

THAT'S WONDERFUL.

I THOUGHT YOU WOULD BE HAPPIER, ELIZABETH. WASN'T IT ALWAYS YOUR DREAM TO LIVE IN FRANCE?

YES, BUT I WANT TO CONTINUE MY VOCAL STUDIES IN MILAN.

SO CONTINUE. YOU WILL JOIN US DURING THE OFF-SEASON.

YOU MEAN IT?

ALL I WANT IS FOR YOU TO BE HAPPY.

SO MOSES MOVED TO PARIS WHILE ELIZABETH LEFT TO STUDY ABROAD IN MILAN.

MARX WAS LEFT IN THE CARE OF A GOVERNESS WHO TAUGHT HIM TO READ AND WRITE.

HE ALWAYS USED TO GLOAT ABOUT HOW HE STARTED READING AT A YOUNG AGE AND ALWAYS MADE SURE TO EXPRESS HIS LOVE OF READING BOOKS TO ME.

I LIKED READING, TOO, BUT HE NEVER APPROVED OF COMICS. WHENEVER HE SAW ME READING THEM, HE WOULD ALWAYS SAY THE SAME THING IN HIS DEEP GRUFF VOICE WITH HIS THICK RUSSIAN ACCENT--

GARBAGE!

HE HATED COMICS!

HE'D ALWAYS INTERRUPT ME WHILE I WAS READING COMICS, JUST TO TELL ME HOW HE USED TO SNEAK INTO HIS FATHER'S LIBRARY AT NIGHT AND READ CLASSIC NOVELS.
IT ANNOYED THE HELL OUT OF ME. I BEGAN TO WONDER IF HE WAS PURPOSELY TRYING TO DISCOURAGE ME FROM READING ALTOGETHER BECAUSE ALL HE DID WAS GLOAT ABOUT HIS UNDYING LOVE OF LITERATURE.
BUT HE WASN'T GLOATING. HE WAS JUST REMEMBERING ONE OF THE ONLY MOMENTS DURING HIS CHILDHOOD WHEN HE WAS TRULY INNOCENT.

ONE NIGHT, MARX TOLD ME THIS STORY ABOUT HIS PARENTS. HE TOLD IT WITH SUCH PASSION THAT I ALMOST COULDN'T BELIEVE THAT HE WAS THE ONE TELLING IT.
IT WAS AS IF THE SPIRITS OF BOTH MOSES AND ELIZABETH POSSESSED MARX FOR JUST THAT MOMENT IN TIME SO THAT I COULD KNOW.
HE RETURNED TO THE SOVIET UNION TO DO HIS PART AND MANAGED TO BRING MANY GERMAN JEWS TO RUSSIA IN ORDER TO PROTECT THEM FROM HITLER'S GROWING INFLUENCE.
IN 1933, MOSES MOVED HIS FAMILY BACK TO THE CITY OF KHARKOV. HE WAS A COMMUNIST. AS A JEW WHOSE FAMILY HAD BEEN PERSECUTED, HE BELIEVED THAT ALL PEOPLE SHOULD BE EQUAL, REGARDLESS OF RELIGION OR STATURE.
ELIZABETH WAS A TRAINED OPERA SINGER. ONCE HER STUDIES ABROAD WERE COMPLETE, SHE BECAME A VERY POPULAR PERFORMER IN KHARKOV.
MOSES USED TO INVITE HIS COLLEAGUES FROM WORK OVER FOR DINNER. THEY WOULD KEEP A BOTTLE OF WINE OUT WHILE PLAYING MUSIC TOGETHER ALL NIGHT.
BUT THEY NEVER GOT AROUND TO OPENING THAT BOTTLE OF WINE BECAUSE, AFTER THE MUSIC WAS DONE, THEY DISCUSSED POLITICS AS IF IT WAS THEIR JOB.
WE WORK TO PROVIDE FOR OUR COUNTRY, NOT JUST OURSELVES. MONEY IS NOTHING MORE THAN MATERIAL THAT TAINTS OUR SOULS.
I AGREE! THERE IS NO FUTURE IN CAPITALISM. THAT'S WHY THE SYSTEM IS FAILING IN AMERICA.
MARX CLAIMED THAT HE BELIEVED IN THE IDEALS OF COMMUNISM, BUT I THINK HE JUST ADMIRED HIS FATHER AND RESPECTED HIS BELIEFS.
HE NEVER HAD A CHANCE TO TALK POLITICS WITH MOSES. HE JUST LISTENED.

DEDUSHKA, WHAT WAS THE POINT OF THE STORY?
WHAT YOU MEAN? THIS IS POINT!

WHEN I WAS BOY, I LISTEN. NEVER TALK. ALL YOU DO NOW IS TALK. TALKING. TALKING. TALKING.

SILENCE IS GOLDEN. LOOSE TONGUE IS *KAKASHKA!*
MY GRANDPA HAD A WAY WITH WORDS. IN RUSSIAN, *KAKASHKA* MEANS SHIT.

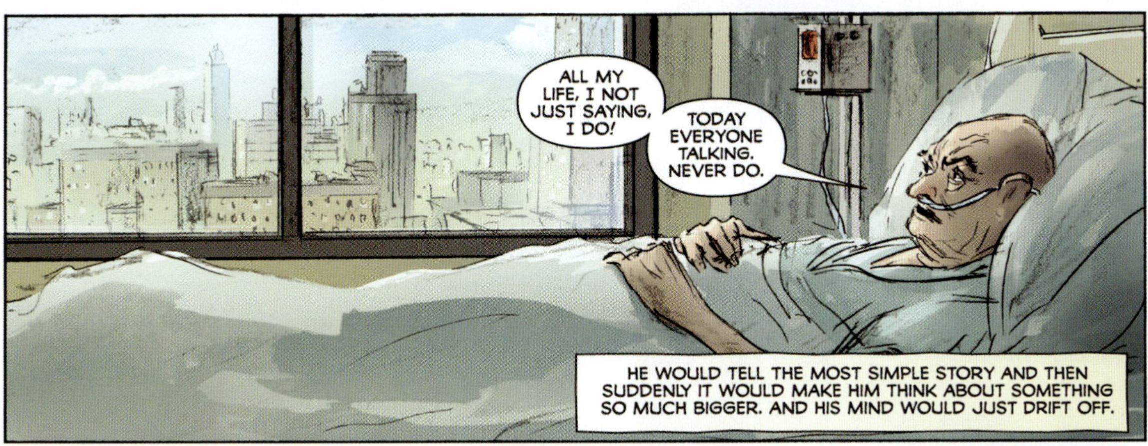
ALL MY LIFE, I NOT JUST SAYING, I DO!
TODAY EVERYONE TALKING. NEVER DO.
HE WOULD TELL THE MOST SIMPLE STORY AND THEN SUDDENLY IT WOULD MAKE HIM THINK ABOUT SOMETHING SO MUCH BIGGER. AND HIS MIND WOULD JUST DRIFT OFF.

IT TOOK A LOT OF EFFORT FOR HIM TO FOCUS ON THE THINGS THAT I NEEDED TO KNOW ABOUT HIS PAST.
OR MAYBE HE WAS FOCUSING TOO MUCH. I WAS TERRIBLE AT READING HIM.

SO...UHM... TELL ME MORE ABOUT YOUR MOTHER.
WHAT YOU WANT TO KNOW?

SHE WAS FAMOUS OPERA SINGER. SHE SING *CARMEN.* SHE SING *MADAM BUTTERFLY.* THIS IS IT.
DID YOU EVER HEAR HER SING?

YES, BUT I NOT FIND INTERESTING.
THAT'S ALL HE EVER TOLD ME.
I'M BORED. LET'S GET OUT OF HERE, MISHA!
I CAN'T, MARX! IF MY FATHER FINDS OUT, HE'LL BEAT ME!

HE WON'T FIND OUT. *TRUST ME.* WE'LL BE BACK BEFORE THE SHOW IS OVER.
HOW WILL WE KNOW IF WE'RE OUTSIDE?
SIMPLE. ONCE THE MUSIC STOPS AND WE HEAR EVERYONE CLAP, WE'LL JUST RUN BACK INSIDE.

WHERE DID YOU GET THOSE!
I STOLE THEM FROM MY FATHER'S BEDROOM.

COUGH COUGH COUGH THESE ARE DISGUSTING!
COUGH COUGH COUGH I THINK YOU JUST NEED TO KEEP PUFFING AND IT GETS EASIER.
NO WAY! I'M DONE WITH THIS!

WHAT THE HELL ARE YOU TWO DOING OUT HERE?!
ARE THOSE CIGARETTES YOU'RE SMOKING?! YOU'RE BOTH IN DEEP TROUBLE!
PAPA!
MARX WAS NOTORIOUS FOR GETTING INTO TROUBLE AS A KID.

AND SO THE PEOPLE RALLIED AGAINST THE TSAR UNDER THE LEADERSHIP OF THE GREAT VLADIMIR LENIN.
WATCH THIS!
NOW WE WILL MOVE ON TO ARITHMETIC. EVERYONE TAKE OUT YOUR BOOKS.
AHHH!
HA
HA
HA
HA
HA
HA
HA
HA
HA!
IT'S HARD TO BELIEVE THAT THE SAME PERSON WHO USED TO CRITICIZE ME FOR PLAYING VIDEOGAMES AND READING COMIC BOOKS BEHAVED LIKE THIS.
AND THIS IS NOTHING COMPARED TO SOME OF THE OTHER PRANKS HE USED TO PULL ON HIS TEACHERS.

AHHHHHH!
IF I EVER PULLED SOMETHING LIKE THIS, MY DAD WOULD HAVE KICKED MY ASS AND GROUNDED ME FOR AT LEAST A DECADE.
BUT I'VE GOT TO HAND IT TO HIM. MARX KNEW HOW TO PISS PEOPLE OFF. *LITERALLY.*

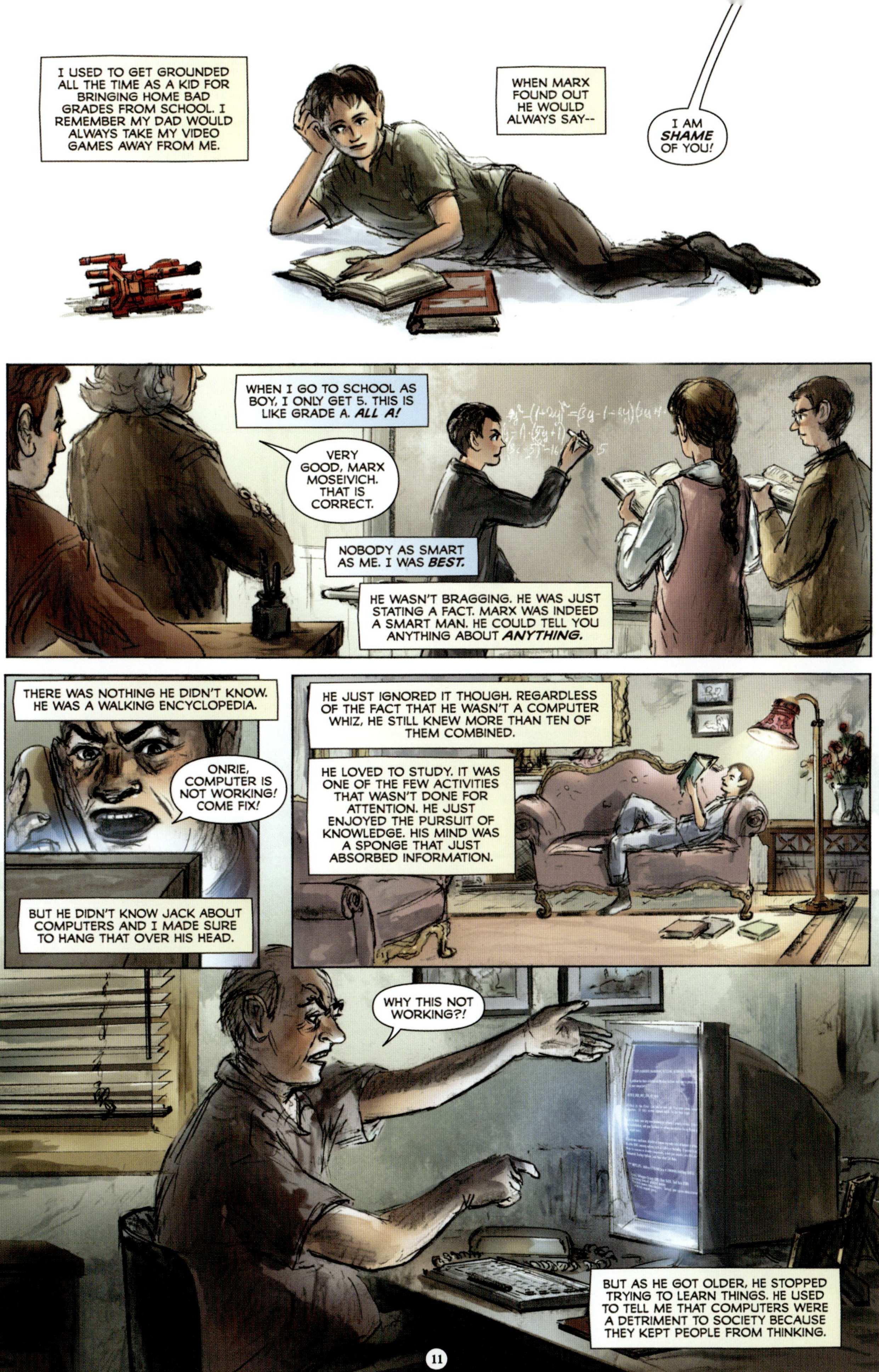

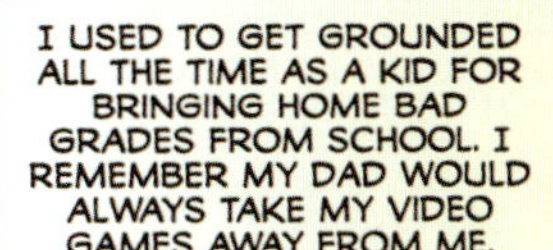

THERE WAS NOTHING HE DIDN'T KNOW. HE WAS A WALKING ENCYCLOPEDIA.

ONRIE, COMPUTER IS NOT WORKING! COME FIX!

BUT HE DIDN'T KNOW JACK ABOUT COMPUTERS AND I MADE SURE TO HANG THAT OVER HIS HEAD.

HE JUST IGNORED IT THOUGH. REGARDLESS OF THE FACT THAT HE WASN'T A COMPUTER WHIZ, HE STILL KNEW MORE THAN TEN OF THEM COMBINED.

HE LOVED TO STUDY. IT WAS ONE OF THE FEW ACTIVITIES THAT WASN'T DONE FOR ATTENTION. HE JUST ENJOYED THE PURSUIT OF KNOWLEDGE. HIS MIND WAS A SPONGE THAT JUST ABSORBED INFORMATION.

WHY THIS NOT WORKING?!

BUT AS HE GOT OLDER, HE STOPPED TRYING TO LEARN THINGS. HE USED TO TELL ME THAT COMPUTERS WERE A DETRIMENT TO SOCIETY BECAUSE THEY KEPT PEOPLE FROM THINKING.

I ONCE ASKED HIM IF ANYONE DISCIPLINED HIM AS A CHILD.
MY BABUSHKA TRY BUT I NOT LISTEN.
I'M NOT HUNGRY.
THAT DOESN'T MATTER. EAT YOUR KASHA.

IT SMELLS BAD. CAN I PUT SOME JELLY ON IT?
NO!
I SAID EAT.
PLEASE?

ALL I KNOW OF MARX'S GRAND-MOTHER IS THAT HE DROVE HER ABSOLUTELY CRAZY.
FINE. I'LL GIVE YOU SOME JELLY BUT IF YOU REFUSE TO EAT AFTER THAT I WILL SLAP YOUR LOBE!
OKAY, BABUSHKA!

DEDUSHKA, YOU NEED TO EAT.
I NOT HUNGRY.
I DON'T EAT THIS BULLSHIT!
TO BE HONEST, THERE WERE TIMES WE ALL FELT THIS WAY.

THIS IS GOING TO TASTE SO MUCH BETTER NOW!

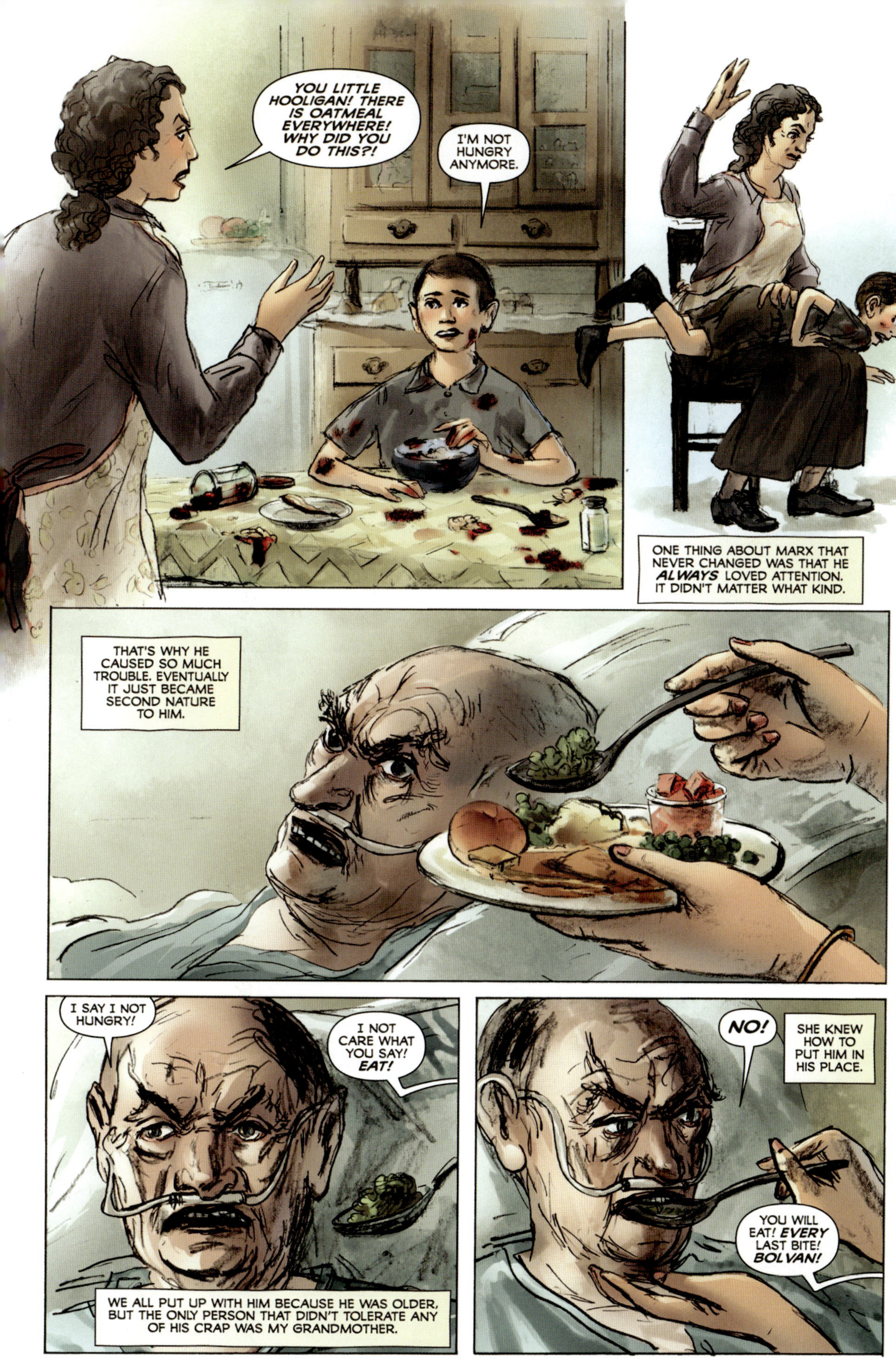

YOU LITTLE HOOLIGAN! THERE IS OATMEAL EVERYWHERE! WHY DID YOU DO THIS?!

I'M NOT HUNGRY ANYMORE.

ONE THING ABOUT MARX THAT NEVER CHANGED WAS THAT HE *ALWAYS* LOVED ATTENTION. IT DIDN'T MATTER WHAT KIND.

THAT'S WHY HE CAUSED SO MUCH TROUBLE. EVENTUALLY IT JUST BECAME SECOND NATURE TO HIM.

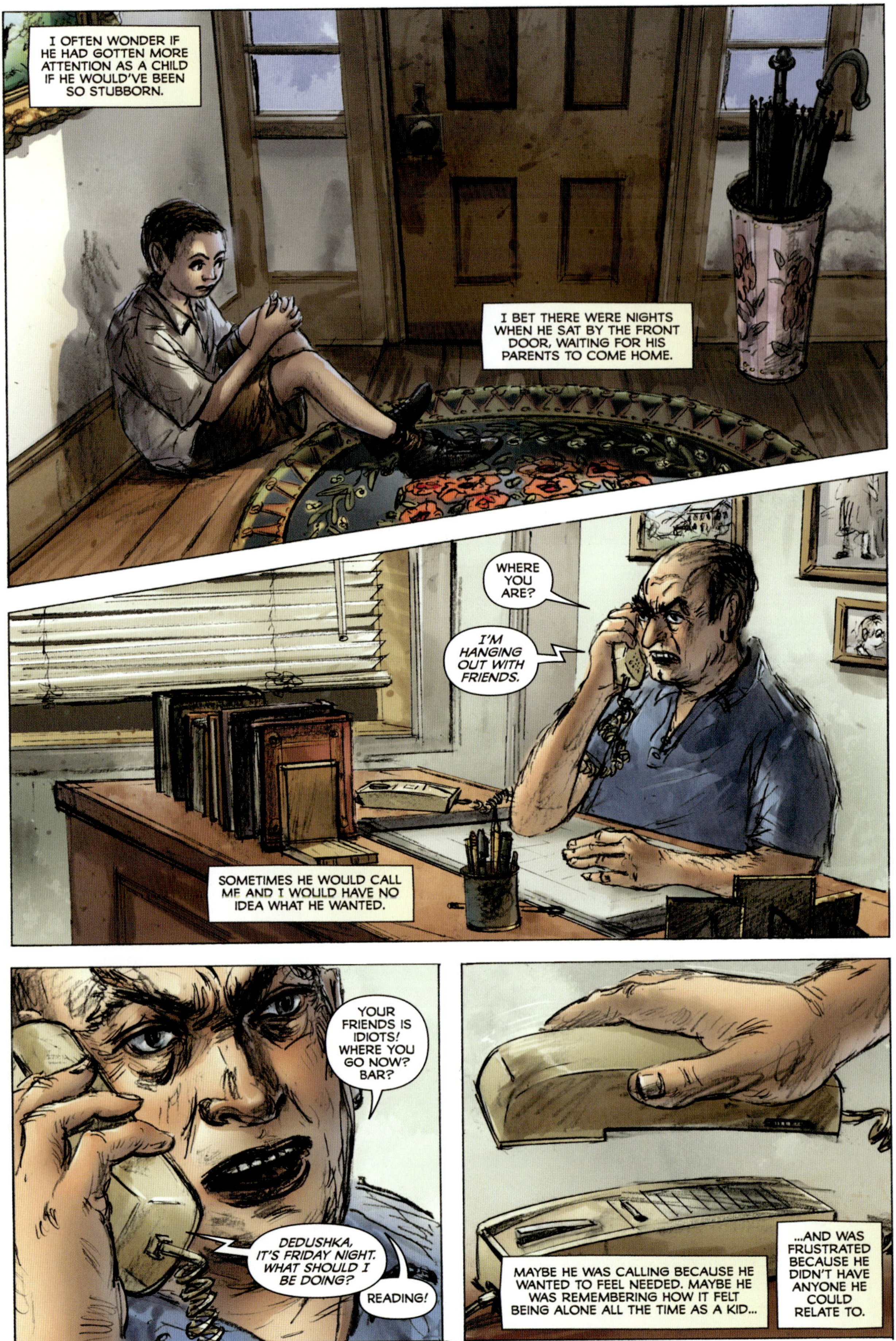

I OFTEN WONDER IF HE HAD GOTTEN MORE ATTENTION AS A CHILD IF HE WOULD'VE BEEN SO STUBBORN.

I BET THERE WERE NIGHTS WHEN HE SAT BY THE FRONT DOOR, WAITING FOR HIS PARENTS TO COME HOME.

WHERE YOU ARE?

I'M HANGING OUT WITH FRIENDS.

SOMETIMES HE WOULD CALL ME AND I WOULD HAVE NO IDEA WHAT HE WANTED.

I THINK THAT'S WHY MARX ALWAYS LOVED ANIMALS. THEY WERE THE ONLY CREATURES IN THIS WORLD THAT HE *COULD* RELATE TO.
ANIMALS, HE ALWAYS SAID, COULD NEVER BE HELD ACCOUNTABLE FOR THEIR ACTIONS.
HE PROBABLY ADMIRED THEM BECAUSE OF IT.
FU! THAT DOG SMELLS LIKE SHIT!
I'M SURE YOU'D SMELL LIKE SHIT, TOO, IF YOU LIVED ON THE STREET, MISHA.
NO, I WOULDN'T.
FINE. I BET YOU THAT I CAN BRING THIS DOG HOME WITH ME AND AFTER A WEEK HE'LL SMELL BETTER THAN YOU.
FINE!
WHOEVER WINS GETS FIVE CIGARETTES PLUS ONE RUBLE!
DEAL!
COME ON, BOY! LET'S GO.
HA, HE'S NOT EVEN FOLLOWING YOU!
THAT'S OKAY--
I'LL JUST CARRY HIM HOME.
GROSS!
SHUT UP!

MARX, IS THAT YOU?!
YES, BABUSHKA!

GO HIDE OVER THERE! QUICKLY!
WHOM ARE YOU TALKING TO?

NOBODY! CAN I GO TO MY ROOM PLEASE?

YOUR TEACHER JUST PAID ME A VISIT. SHE TOLD ME THAT YOU DUMPED URINE OVER HER HEAD YESTERDAY!

WHAT IS THAT SMELL? IT SMELLS LIKE--LIKE--

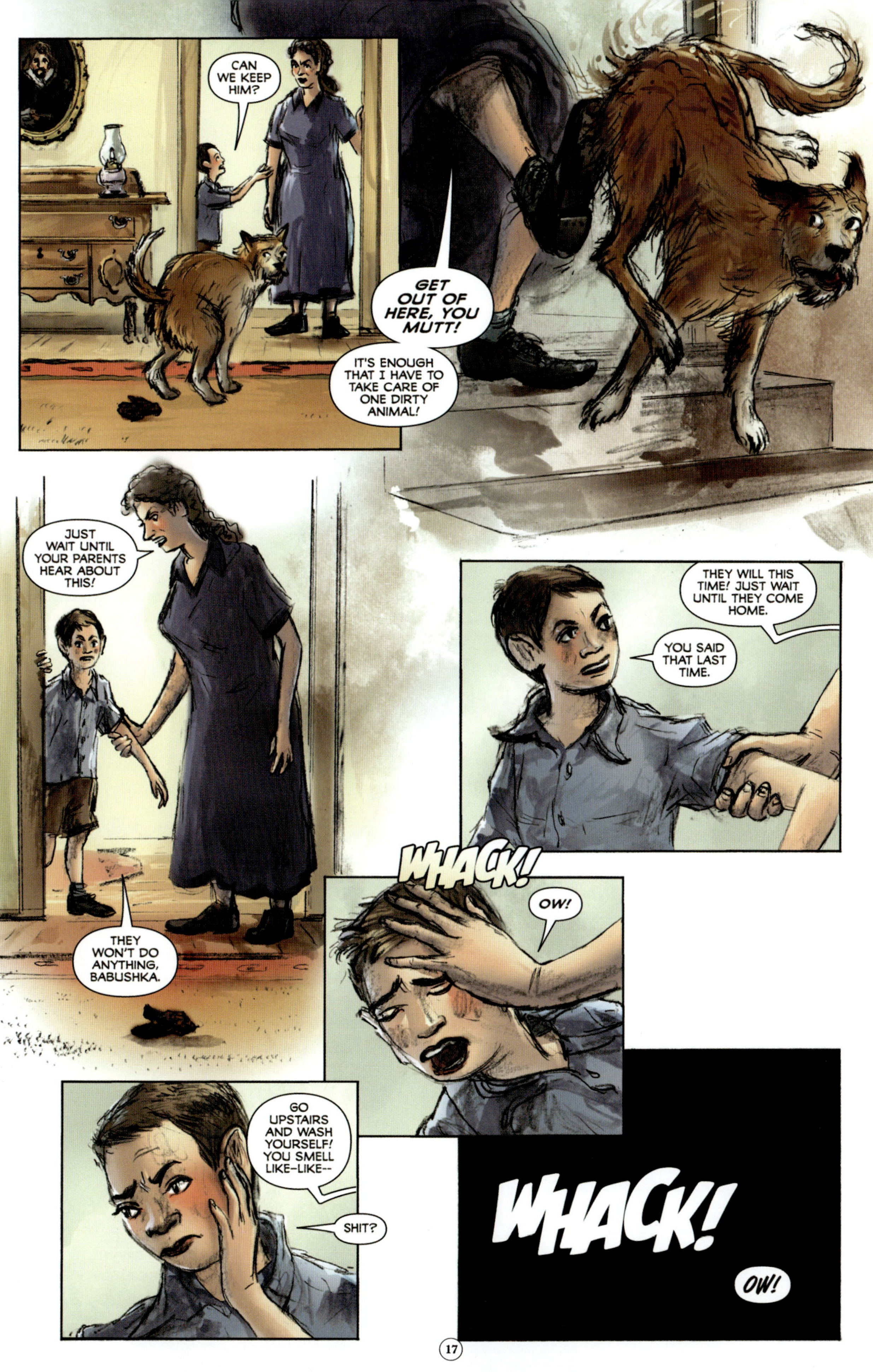
CAN WE KEEP HIM?
GET OUT OF HERE, YOU MUTT!
IT'S ENOUGH THAT I HAVE TO TAKE CARE OF ONE DIRTY ANIMAL!
JUST WAIT UNTIL YOUR PARENTS HEAR ABOUT THIS!
THEY WON'T DO ANYTHING, BABUSHKA.
THEY WILL THIS TIME! JUST WAIT UNTIL THEY COME HOME.
YOU SAID THAT LAST TIME.
WHACK!
OW!
GO UPSTAIRS AND WASH YOURSELF! YOU SMELL LIKE--LIKE--
SHIT?
WHACK!
OW!

I DON'T KNOW WHETHER OR NOT MARX, MOSES AND ELIZABETH EVER SAT DOWN FOR SOMETHING AS COMMON AS A FAMILY DINNER.
MOSES, I HAVE SOMETHING TO TELL YOU.
MMM?
I'M PREGNANT.
THAT'S WONDERFUL!
I'M GOING TO HAVE A BROTHER!
WHAT I DO KNOW IS THAT THIS IS THE POINT WHEN MARX'S LIFE CHANGED FOREVER.

MARX USED TO BEG MY GRANDMOTHER TO TELL HIM THREE SIMPLE WORDS, "I LOVE YOU." HE WANTED TO HEAR IT EVERY DAY. EVENTUALLY SHE JUST STARTED TELLING HIM TO SHUT UP.

SHE COULDN'T STAND HIS NEED FOR CONSTANT ATTENTION.

YOUR MOTHER IS TIRED! GO OUTSIDE AND PLAY!

WE ALL BELIEVE THAT MARX WAS LIKE THIS BECAUSE FEW PEOPLE EVER TOLD HIM WHAT HE REALLY NEEDED TO HEAR.

MY GRANDMOTHER JUST ROLLED HER EYES. SHE WOULD SAY "HE NEEDS A MOTHER!" IN A VERY SHARP TONE.

EVER SINCE MARX PASSED AWAY, MY GRANDMOTHER REMEMBERS THIS AND IT BRINGS TEARS TO HER EYES EVERY TIME.

ALL SHE WANTED TO DO IS SAY I LOVE YOU TO HIM JUST ONE MORE TIME...

...AND SEE HIM LIGHT UP WITH JOY.

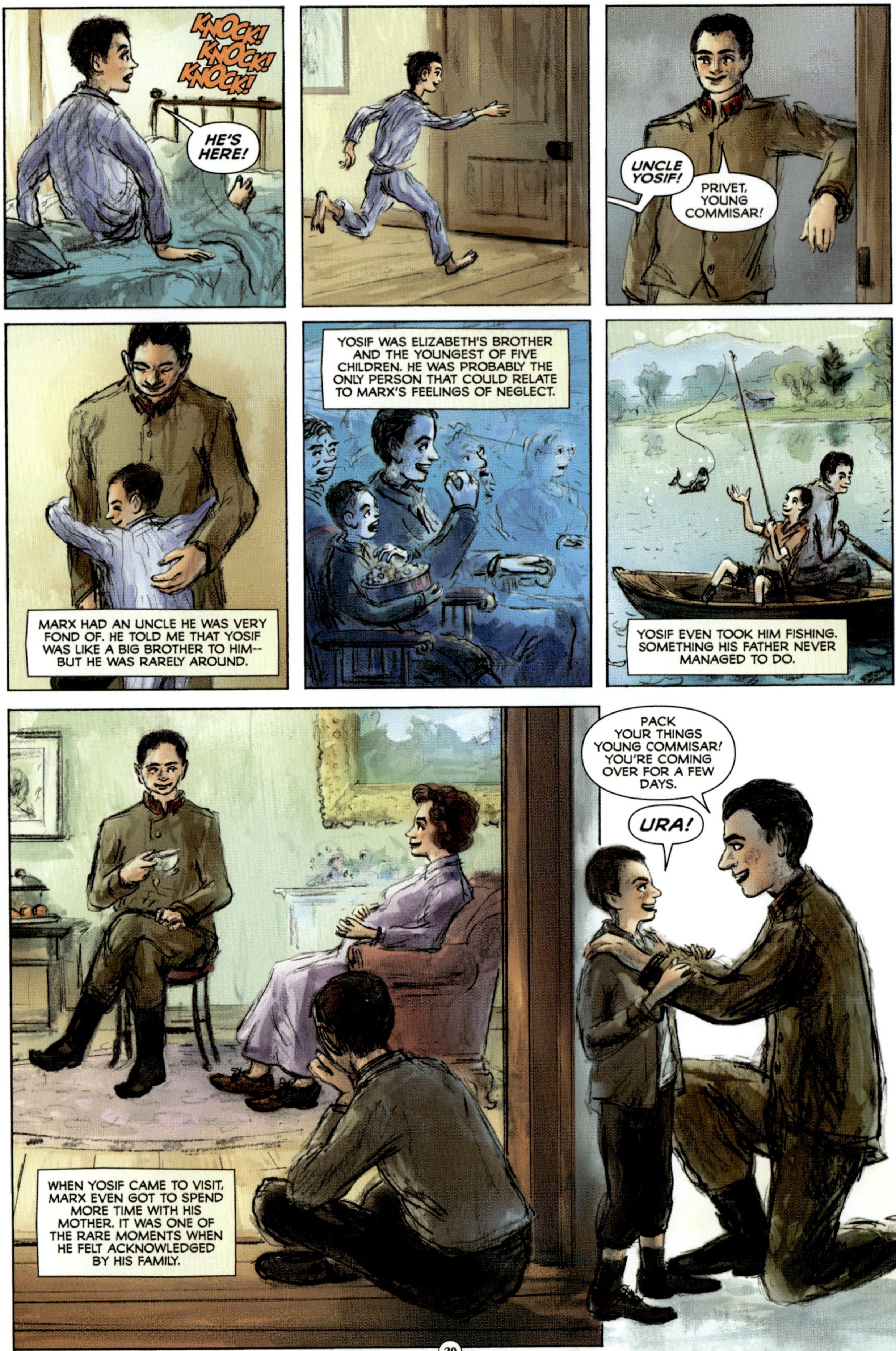

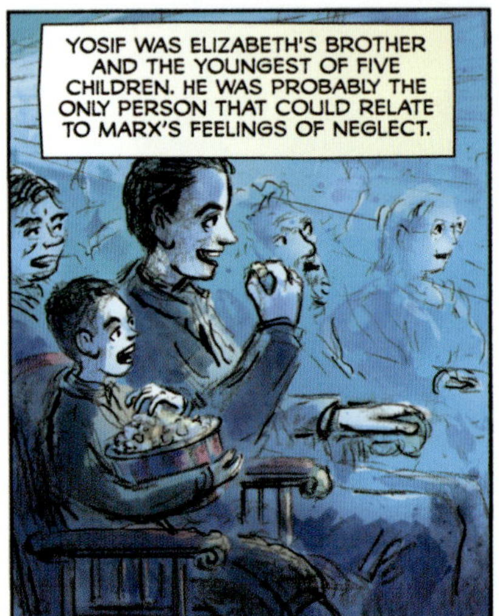

WHEN YOSIF CAME TO VISIT, MARX EVEN GOT TO SPEND MORE TIME WITH HIS MOTHER. IT WAS ONE OF THE RARE MOMENTS WHEN HE FELT ACKNOWLEDGED BY HIS FAMILY.

PACK YOUR THINGS YOUNG COMMISAR! YOU'RE COMING OVER FOR A FEW DAYS.

URA!

AUGUST 1933.
MARX, GET DRESSED RIGHT NOW!
WE HAVE TO GO. QUICKLY!
WHAT'S GOING ON?
WHERE ARE WE GOING, UNCLE YOSIF?
TO THE HOSPITAL. TO SEE YOUR MOTHER.
IS MY BABY BROTHER BORN YET?
UNCLE YOSIF?
YOU'LL FIND OUT SOON, MARX. KEEP UP WITH ME.

STAY RIGHT HERE.

MARX...

YOUR MOTHER ISN'T WITH US ANYMORE.

SHE DIED IN CHILDBIRTH ALONG WITH YOUR BABY SISTER.

I'M SO SORRY.

I ONCE ASKED MARX IF HE CRIED ON THE DAY HIS MOTHER DIED. HE NEVER ANSWERED.

CHAPTER 2:

ORPHAN

HOW DID YOUR FATHER DIE?
WHY YOU WANT TO KNOW?
BECAUSE IT'S IMPORTANT FOR MY STORY.
WHAT STORY YOU WRITE? YOUR STORY IS GARBAGE!
MY STORY IS ABOUT YOU!
WHY YOU WRITE STORY ABOUT ME?
LOOK, EITHER TELL ME ABOUT YOUR FATHER OR I'M LEAVING.
OKAY, OKAY. I TELL YOU SOMETHING.

KHARKOV, 1934.
GOOD MORNING, DR. MELNIK.
GOOD MORNING, GRIGORI.
MY FATHER FAMOUS MICROBIOLOGIST. HE MAKE LESS MONEY THAN DRIVER.
HE EARNED LESS MONEY THAN HIS DRIVER? HOW COULD HE AFFORD HIM THEN?
METCHNIKOFF INSTITUTE PAY DRIVER.
THEY PAID THEIR OWN DRIVERS MORE THAN THEIR MICROBIOLOGISTS? THAT SOUNDS STUPID.
IS NOT STUPID! MONEY IS STUPID! MY FATHER HATE MONEY. ALL YOU AMERICANS TALK ABOUT IS MONEY, MONEY, MONEY!
HMPH! STALIN IS OUT OF CONTROL. I HAVE NO IDEA HOW THE PEOPLE STAND FOR THIS.
DR. MELNIK, YOU SHOULDN'T SAY SUCH THINGS.
I HEARD A LOCAL POSTMAN WAS ARRESTED THE OTHER DAY FOR SIMPLY COMMENTING ON THE WAY COMRADE STALIN DRESSES.
THAT'S RIDICULOUS! STALIN IS A SERVANT OF THE PEOPLE. NOT THE OTHER WAY AROUND.
YOU HAVEN'T BEEN YOURSELF SINCE MRS. MELNIK PASSED AWAY.
MAYBE YOU SHOULD LOOK INTO GETTING MARRIED. FIND SOMEONE TO TAKE CARE OF YOUNG MARX.
I'M ALREADY GETTING MARRIED, GRIGORI.
HER NAME IS NINA KLUEVA. SHE IS ONE OF THE BEST MICROBIOLOGISTS IN THE FIELD.
SOUNDS LIKE A MATCH MADE IN HEAVEN!
MY FATHER WORKING AT KHARKOV MECHNIKOFF INSTITUTE. HE WAS VERY IMPORTANT.
WHAT DID HE DO THERE?
HE WAS DIRECTOR OF INSTITUTE. STALIN KILL HIM WHEN I WAS THIRTEEN.

NINA, THIS IS MY SON, MARX. I'LL LET YOU TWO GET TO KNOW EACH OTHER. I'M GOING BACK TO WORK.
I ALMOST NOT SEE HIM EVER. WHEN MY MOTHER DIE, MY FATHER MARRY NEW WOMAN AND THAT'S IT.
DID YOU LIKE HER?
YES. I LOVE HER VERY MUCH.
PLEASED TO MEET YOU, NINA GEORGIVNA.
IT'S NICE TO MEET YOU TOO, MARX.
YOU ARE SUCH A WELL-MANNERED BOY.
DON'T LET HIM FOOL YOU.
THE BOY IS AN *ASS* WITH *EARS!*
SO YOUR GRANDMOTHER TOOK CARE OF YOU AFTER YOUR MOTHER DIED?
YES. NINA ALSO WORKING VERY MUCH. SHE NOT HAVE TIME TO SIT WITH ME.
THIS IS WHAT YOU GET FOR PUTTING MUD IN THE CAKE MIX.
THIS IS WHAT YOU GET FOR WALKING AROUND THE HOUSE IN DIRTY SHOES AGAIN!
THIS IS WHAT YOU GET FOR WASHING MEAT IN TOILET WATER!
I CAUSE MANY TROUBLE FOR MY BABUSHKA.

DID YOU FATHER WORK CLOSELY WITH NINA?
THEY WORK IN SAME PLACE BUT MY FATHER BUSY WITH OTHER THINGS.
STALIN IS IMPRISONING THE JEWISH SCHOLARS THAT I BROUGHT HERE FROM GERMANY SIMPLY BECAUSE HE THINKS THEY ARE TOO EDUCATED! THIS IS MADNESS!
DR. MELNIK, YOU SERVE YOUR COUNTRY VERY WELL. WE ADVISE THAT YOU FOCUS MORE ON YOUR WORK AND LESS ON THE ACTIVITIES OF COMRADE STALIN.
HOW DO YOU EXPECT ME TO FOCUS ON MY WORK WHEN THE PEOPLE I WORK WITH AREN'T SAFE? GET OUT OF MY OFFICE!
KHARKOV, 1937.
THE GREAT VLADIMIR LENIN DIED OF A HEART ATTACK IN 1924 AND SINCE THEN JOSEPH STALIN HAS BEEN APPOINTED AS THE--
GENERAL SECRETARY OF THE COMMUNIST PARTY OF THE SOVIET UNION.
WHILE MY FATHER WORKING, I GO TO SCHOOL.
VERY GOOD, MARX MOSEIVICH.
WHEN I WAS THIRTEEN, I MEET MY FIRST WIFE, ELENA SABOTSKIYA.

MARX, WHAT ARE YOU DOING THIS SATURDAY NIGHT?
STUDYING.
THAT IS ALL YOU EVER DO. COME ON-- TAKE ME OUT ON A DATE!
THIS SATURDAY? BUT I HAVE TO--
GREAT! I'LL SEE YOU THEN!
MARX RARELY SPOKE ABOUT ELENA. THE WAY HE ALWAYS LOOKED AT MY GRANDMOTHER, WITH SUCH LOVING EYES, IT WAS HARD TO BELIEVE THAT ANYONE COULD HAVE COME BEFORE HER.
WHEN I ASKED HIM IF HE EVER LOVED ELENA, HE SAID,
"WHAT MATTER? SHE WAS GOOD PERSON."

BABUSHKA! I'M HOME!
HELLO?
I'M IN THE KITCHEN!
DON'T BOTHER GETTING UNDRESSED. I NEED YOU TO BRING YOUR FATHER SOMETHING TO EAT.
HE HASN'T BEEN HOME IN *DAYS.*
MAKE SURE THAT HE EATS! EVERY LAST BITE!

DO YOU THINK MOSES KNEW THAT HE WAS IN TROUBLE?
OF COURSE.
MY FATHER NOT STUPID.
HE KNEW IT WAS TOO LATE.
IT WAS JUST MATTER OF TIME.
YULIA, THIS IS FOR NINA. PLEASE MAKE SURE SHE RECEIVES IT. DO YOU UNDERSTAND?
YES, DR. MELNIK.
YOU SHOULD GO HOME NOW.

PAPA?
BABUSHKA IS WORRIED ABOUT YOU. SHE MADE YOU SOMETHING TO EAT.
OH--
MY FATHER WORKED SO MUCH THAT HE FAINTED WHILE HE WAS AT HIS DESK. HE NOT EAT FOR DAYS.
THAT WAS LAST TIME I SEE HIM.

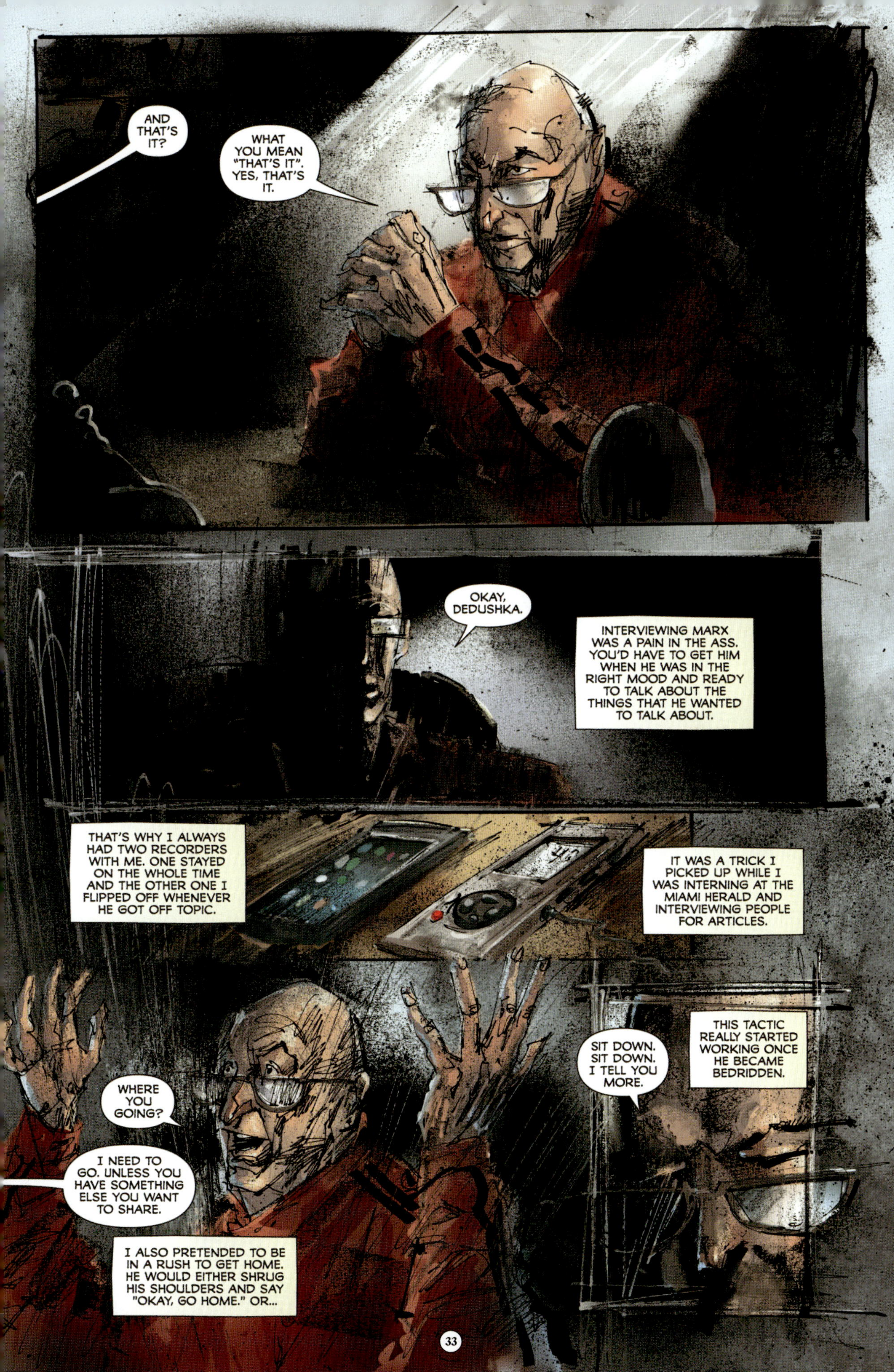
AND THAT'S IT?
WHAT YOU MEAN "THAT'S IT". YES, THAT'S IT.
OKAY, DEDUSHKA.
INTERVIEWING MARX WAS A PAIN IN THE ASS. YOU'D HAVE TO GET HIM WHEN HE WAS IN THE RIGHT MOOD AND READY TO TALK ABOUT THE THINGS THAT HE WANTED TO TALK ABOUT.
THAT'S WHY I ALWAYS HAD TWO RECORDERS WITH ME. ONE STAYED ON THE WHOLE TIME AND THE OTHER ONE I FLIPPED OFF WHENEVER HE GOT OFF TOPIC.
IT WAS A TRICK I PICKED UP WHILE I WAS INTERNING AT THE MIAMI HERALD AND INTERVIEWING PEOPLE FOR ARTICLES.
WHERE YOU GOING?
I NEED TO GO. UNLESS YOU HAVE SOMETHING ELSE YOU WANT TO SHARE.
I ALSO PRETENDED TO BE IN A RUSH TO GET HOME. HE WOULD EITHER SHRUG HIS SHOULDERS AND SAY "OKAY, GO HOME." OR...
SIT DOWN. SIT DOWN. I TELL YOU MORE.
THIS TACTIC REALLY STARTED WORKING ONCE HE BECAME BEDRIDDEN.

WAKE UP!
MY FATHER ALWAYS SPEAK HIS MIND. ONE DAY, THEY ARREST HIM.
WHAT IS THE MEANING OF THIS?
MOSES MELNIK, YOU'RE UNDER ARREST.
I'M NOT GOING ANYWHERE UNTIL YOU TELL ME WHO SENT YOU!
THIS WHAT STALIN DID. HE KILL EVERYONE. NO MATTER WHO. GOOD PERSON. BAD PERSON. IS NOT MATTER.

STALIN ORDER ALL MY FATHER'S RESEARCH ON TYPHOID TO BE DESTROYED. HE ALSO STRIP HIM OF POSITION AS DIRECTOR OF METCHNIKOFF INSTITUTE.
HE MAKE MY FATHER DISAPPEAR.
MY FATHER WROTE MANY BOOKS. IN RUSSIAN, IN FRENCH, EVEN ENGLISH. ALL OF THEM NOW GONE.
I SPENT MANY YEAR LOOKING FOR COPY. I FIND ONLY LITTLE SCRAPS.
EVERYTHING GONE.

YOU'RE MAKING A MISTAKE! I'M AN *INNOCENT* MAN!
YES, YES, YOU ALL SAY THAT YOU'RE INNOCENT. NOBODY GIVES A SHIT!
KEEP WALKING YOU FUCKING TRAITOR!
I AM NOT A TRAITOR! STALIN IS A--
BLAM BLAM
NOBODY REALLY KNOWS HOW MOSES MELNIK WAS MURDERED.
IT HURTS ME DEEPLY TO THINK THAT MY GREAT GRANDFATHER SACRIFICED HIS LIFE FOR SOMETHING HE BELIEVED IN ONLY TO HAVE IT ALL TAKEN AWAY FROM HIM.
HIS FAMILY. HIS HONOR. HIS LIFE.
ALL FOR THE SOVIET UNION.

WHEN THEY TAKE MY FATHER AWAY, NKVD SEND MY BABUSHKA LETTER.
WHAT DID IT SAY?
IT SAY THAT MY FATHER WAS "ENEMY OF THE STATE."
I REMEMBER MY FATHER GAVE ME VERY SPECIAL PEN. TODAY, THEY DO NOT MAKE PEN LIKE THIS NO MORE.
HE ALWAYS USE IT. HE SAY TO ME THAT PEN IS STRONGER THAN BULLET.
MARX NEVER ADMITTED TO CRYING. EVER. BUT I CAN'T IMAGINE HOW HE COULDN'T HAVE CRIED ON THE DAY HIS FATHER VANISHED WITHOUT A TRACE...
...NEVER TO BE SEEN OR HEARD FROM AGAIN.
MARX?
YOU POOR CHILD.
WHEN MY FATHER DIE, MY STEP-MOTHER TAKE ME TO MOSCOW WITH HER. MY BABUSHKA WAS OLD AND TIRED.
MY FATHER ASK NINA TO MAKE SURE THAT I HAVE GOOD EDUCATION.

ELENA! WHAT ARE YOU DOING HERE?
WE MADE PLANS TO GO OUT TONIGHT! DON'T YOU REMEMBER?
I CAN'T GO OUT TONIGHT. I'M LEAVING IN TWO DAYS.
WHERE?
MOSCOW. AND I DON'T THINK I'LL BE COMING BACK.
WHY?
I'M GOING TO A NEW SCHOOL.
SO THEN WE'LL NEVER SEE EACH OTHER AGAIN?
I DON'T KNOW. MAYBE.
I'M GOING TO WORRY ABOUT YOU ALL THE TIME. WRITE TO ME!
WRITE TO YOU? OKAY, I SUPPOSE I--
MARX WAS ALWAYS LOYAL. IF HE AGREED TO DO SOMETHING, HE DID IT. EVEN IF IT WASN'T SOMETHING HE NECESSARILY WANTED TO DO.

MOSCOW, 1937.
NINA TAKE ME TO MOSCOW. FAR AWAY FROM KHARKOV. SHE TAKE NEW JOB AND SEND ME TO NEW SCHOOL.
WHEN MY FATHER DIE, SHE TAKING CARE OF ME.
MARX, THIS IS MY FATHER. YOU WILL BE LIVING WITH US FROM NOW ON.
NOW LISTEN HERE, BOY--
--THE RULES HERE ARE VERY SIMPLE. YOU COOK, YOU CLEAN, YOU GO TO SCHOOL, YOU DO YOUR HOMEWORK--
--AND YOU ARE IN THIS APARTMENT EVERY NIGHT BEFORE 2200 HOURS. IF YOU COME HOME ANY LATER THE DOOR WILL BE LOCKED. UNDERSTOOD?
HE SOUNDED STRICT. YOU MUST HAVE HATED LIVING LIKE THAT.
I NOT HATE! I RESPECT! HE VERY SMART MAN.

EVEN BEFORE HE WAS SENT OFF TO WAR, MARX WAS CONDITIONED FOR MILITARY LIFE.
ITS NO WONDER MY GRANDFATHER ENDED UP BEING SUCH A STICKLER FOR PROMPTNESS.
HE ALWAYS STRESSED THE IMPORTANCE OF BEING ON TIME.
HE WAS NEVER LATE. FOR ANYTHING.
RIGHT ON TIME.
IT'S HOW HE KEPT HIMSELF IN CONTROL. HE ALWAYS FOCUSED ON WHAT WAS IN FRONT OF HIM.

I LIVE VERY WELL WITH NINA AND GEORGEI. I STUDY.
I WORKING. I WAS BEST AT CLEANING!
I HAVE NEVER SEEN ANYONE CLEAN SO SLOPPY. GO OVER THE FLOORS AGAIN!
AND EVERY NIGHT I COME HOME AT 10PM.
I WAS HELD UP AT SCHOOL. WE HAVE EXAMS THIS WEEK.
YOU ARE LUCKY. I ALMOST LOCKED THE DOOR FOR THE NIGHT.
I STOP THINKING ABOUT WHAT HAPPENED TO MY FATHER.
EVERY DAY I EXERCISE. MIND AND BODY MUST ALWAYS BE STRONG.
AT THIS POINT, MARX DIDN'T EVEN KNOW THAT HIS FATHER HAD BEEN KILLED. BUT HE WAS NOW TAKING HIS LIFE A LOT MORE SERIOUSLY.

NO ONE ACTED AGAINST STALIN BECAUSE IF THE THOUGHT EVEN CROSSED YOUR MIND, YOU WOULD ALREADY BE DEAD.
THE ONLY THING TO DO WAS TO SHUT UP AND MIND YOUR OWN BUSINESS--BUT EVEN THAT DIDN'T GUARANTEE YOUR SAFETY.
IGOR! THEY TOOK HIM AWAY!
PLEASE HELP ME! THEY CAME AND THEY TOOK MY HUSBAND!
NOTHING DID.
THERE WAS NO JUSTICE IN THE SOVIET UNION. EVERYONE FEARED FOR THEIR LIVES.
PAPA, I WANT TO GO HOME.
I'M SORRY, SON, BUT WE CAN'T!
NO ONE WAS EVER TRULY SAFE.
WE HAVE TO KEEP MOVING.
OUT OF OUR WAY!
NOBODY OUTRAN THE NKVD.

DID YOU EVER GET INTO FIGHTS?
YES. ONE TIME.
WELL, LOOK WHO IT IS. THE NEW KID!
EVERYONE SAYS YOUR FATHER IS AN ENEMY OF THE STATE.
AND SO ARE YOU!
SO WHAT DID YOU DO?
I BEAT SHIT OUT OF THEM.

ATTENTION! ATTENTION! THIS WORD FROM MOSCOW.
ON THIS MORNING, JUNE 22ND, 1941, THE MOTHERLAND HAS BEEN INVADED BY NAZI GERMANY.

WE NEED TO GET YOU OUT OF MOSCOW!
NO. I WANT TO FIGHT.
BUT I PROMISED YOUR FATHER I WOULD KEEP YOU SAFE.

ENOUGH NINA. MARX IS NO LONGER A BOY. HE IS NOW A MAN.
HE CAN FIGHT HIS OWN BATTLES.

SO MANY BAD THINGS HAVE HAPPENED TO YOU ALREADY! **AND NOW THIS!**

COMRADE STALIN HAS ISSUED AN IMMEDIATE CALL TO ARMS.
THOSE OF YOU-- ZZZT.

I'VE HEARD ENOUGH.

WERE YOU SCARED ABOUT JOINING THE ARMY?
OF COURSE NO! I WANT TO FIGHT NAZIS! THEY KILL OUR PEOPLE!
I SCARED OF NOTHING. IF I DIE, I GO TO BE WITH MY MOTHER AND FATHER.
SOMEONE SENT YOU A LETTER.
ELENA WROTE ME MANY TIME. SHE ALSO DRAFTED INTO THE ARMY. SHE DROP BOMB FROM PLANE.
EVERYONE FIGHTING NAZI. SCARE OR NO.
YOU ARE GOING TO SEE TERRIBLE THINGS OUT THERE. NOTHING YOU'VE EVER HEARD, SEEN OR READ IS GOING TO PREPARE YOU FOR IT.
WAR DOESN'T JUST TAKE LIVES. IT CAN *DESTROY YOUR SOUL* IF YOU LET IT.
JUST REMEMBER ONE THING--
DON'T *EVER* TELL ANYONE YOU'RE SCARED. THAT IS THE ONLY WAY TO SURVIVE.

MARX?
IT'S TIME FOR YOU TO GET READY. YOU DON'T WANT TO MISS THE TRAIN.
HOW DO I LOOK?
LIKE YOUR FATHER.
TAKE CARE OF YOURSELF, SON!
I WILL. I PROMISE.

WERE YOU AFRAID OF JOINING THE ARMY?
NO. I WAS NEVER AFRAID. HITLER WAS BAD PERSON. I WANTED TO KILL HIM.
EVERYONE DID.

NOW I UNDERSTOOD WHY MARX ALWAYS KEPT HIS MIND OCCUPIED.

WHAT ELSE YOU WANT TO KNOW?

I THINK THAT'S ENOUGH FOR TODAY, GRANDPA. WHY DON'T YOU GET SOME REST?

OKAY. YOU COME TOMORROW?

YES.

HIS PAST IS WHAT MADE HIM, BUT THE OLD MAN IN FRONT OF ME WAS THE ONLY MARX I EVER KNEW.

HE ALWAYS SPOKE ABOUT HIS ACTIONS DURING THE WAR WITH SUCH PRIDE. WE WERE ALL BROUGHT UP TO BELIEVE THAT HE NEVER FELT FEAR.

BUT EVERY MAN KNOWS FEAR. SOME ARE JUST BETTER AT HIDING IT THAN OTHERS.

CHAPTER 3:
SOLDIER OF MISFORTUNE

Onrie Kompan
WRITER

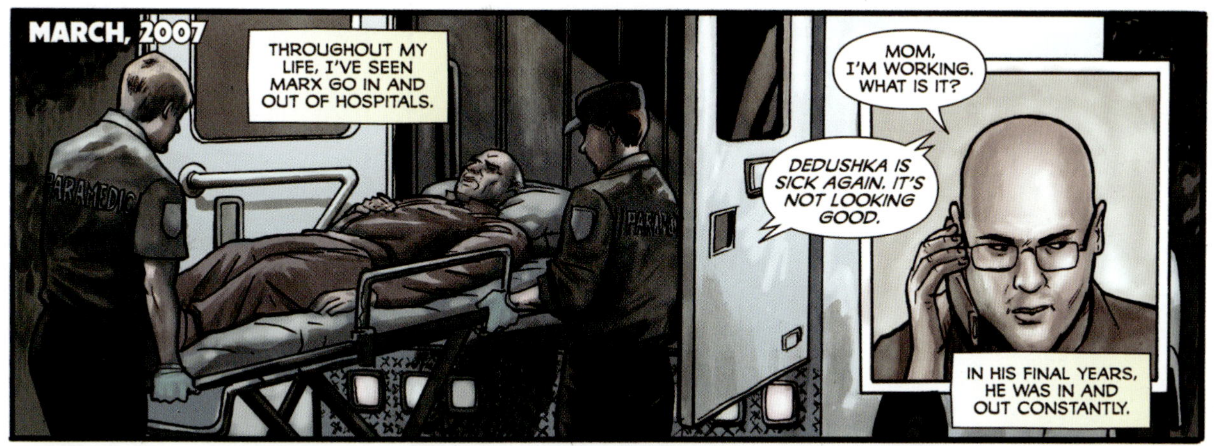
MARCH, 2007
THROUGHOUT MY LIFE, I'VE SEEN MARX GO IN AND OUT OF HOSPITALS.
PARAMEDIC
PARAMED
MOM, I'M WORKING. WHAT IS IT?
DEDUSHKA IS SICK AGAIN. IT'S NOT LOOKING GOOD.
IN HIS FINAL YEARS, HE WAS IN AND OUT CONSTANTLY.

JULY, 2008
BABUSHKA, IT'S MIDNIGHT. WHAT DO YOU WANT?
DEDUSHKA'S BLOOD PRESSURE IS HIGH! TAKE HIM TO EMERGENCY HOSPITAL NOW!
BUT NO MATTER HOW BAD THINGS SEEMED, HE KEPT ON WALKING RIGHT OUT OF THE HOSPITAL.

APRIL, 2009
I SAY I'M FINE! I HAVE RARE COINS COMING IN MAIL TODAY! LET ME GO HOME!
HE HATED BEING IN THE HOSPITAL SO MUCH THAT IT GAVE HIM STRENGTH TO PERSEVERE AND OVERCOME THE ODDS.
DAD, WHY WERE YOU GUYS CALLING ME SO MUCH LAST NIGHT?
YOUR GRANDFATHER IS BACK IN THE HOSPITAL.
AGAIN? I'LL BE RIGHT OVER!

JANUARY, 2010
GRANDMA, WHAT'S WRONG?
CALL THE EMERGENCY! CALL THE EMERGENCY!
OY...OY.
JEANS
DEDUSHKA IS VERY SICK!
YEAR AFTER YEAR HE STUBBORNLY FOUGHT HIS WAY IN AND OUT OF HOSPITALS BUT HIS STRENGTH WAS NOW WEARING THIN.

MAY, 2011
I WAS FOOLED INTO THINKING HE WAS INVINCIBLE AND WAS FINALLY DRAGGED TO REALITY FOUR MONTHS BEFORE HE PASSED AWAY.
Northwestern Memorial Hospital
Galter Pavilion

DURING THE LATER YEARS OF HIS LIFE, MARX BATTLED WITH HIS HEALTH AND ALWAYS MANAGED TO SURVIVE.

IN HIS YOUTH, HE BATTLED NAZIS AND SURVIVED A WAR THAT RESULTED IN THE DEATHS OF MILLIONS.

HOW HE ALWAYS MANAGED TO OVERCOME THE ODDS WAS A TESTAMENT TO HIS DESIRE TO LIVE.

HIS ENTIRE LIFE WAS
A CONSTANT BATTLE
FOR SURVIVAL.

WITHIN HOURS HE WAS SEIZED BY NVKD OFFICERS AND THROWN INTO PRISON.

THEY SLAPPED HIM WITH A TEN-YEAR PRISON TERM AND THEN RELEASED HIM FROM JAIL ONCE THE NAZI INVASION BEGAN.

HE WOULD CARRY OUT THE REST OF HIS SENTENCE ON THE BATTLEFIELD.

MARX'S MILITARY TRAINING LASTED ONLY TWO WEEKS. HE SAID THAT THE OFFICERS THAT TRAINED THE NEW RECRUITS WERE ALL INCOMPETENT.
MANY OF THEM HAD SIMILAR STORIES TO STEPAN.

WHAT'S MORE USELESS THAN A JEW WITH A GUN?
A JEW WITH A BIG NOSE AND A GUN.

I THOUGHT JUDENS WERE ALL AFRAID OF "ZE FUHRER." IF YOU COWARDS ACTUALLY FOUGHT BACK, WE WOULDN'T EVEN BE IN THIS WAR.

STAY OUT OF MY WAY WHEN THE FIGHTING STARTS, JEW.

WHAT THE HELL IS GOING ON HERE?! QUIT HOLDING UP THE *FUCKING* LINE, BIARSKY!

DON'T MIND THOSE *FUCKING* IDIOTS, MELNIK.

THESE RUSSIAN *FUCKS* DON'T LIKE POLLOCKS ANY MORE THAN JEWS. BUT WE'LL SHOW THEM, RIGHT?
YES SIR.

YOU KNOW, MY NEIGHBOR IN LVIV WAS JEWISH. HE HAD FIVE SONS. THEY WERE SMART PEOPLE.
THEY ARE PROBABLY DEAD NOW.
WHY AREN'T YOU EATING?
I'M NOT HUNGRY.
REALLY? WELL, THEN, CAN I HAVE YOUR BOWL?
GO RIGHT AHEAD.

I CAN'T SHOOT STRAIGHT! MY NOSE IS IN THE WAY!
I'LL RAM RIGHT INTO FRITZ AND HIS NAZI BRETHEREN WITH MY JEW HORNS!

AUGUST, 1941.
EVERYONE THAT WAS PLACED INTO OFFICER TRAINING SCHOOL WALKED OUT TWO WEEKS LATER AND WAS SENT TO THE FRONTLINES. MARX REPORTED TO *LIEUTENANT BLECKER.*
YOU MEN ARE NOW OFFICERS OF THE 16TH ARMY, WHICH IS UNDER THE COMMAND OF GENERAL KONSTANTIN ROKOSSOVSKY.

OUR MISSION IS SIMPLE. WE'RE TO REPEL THE NAZI INVASION ON THE WESTERN FRONT.

EACH UNIT WILL BE ASSIGNED FOUR FULLY ARMED GAZ-AAA TRUCKS.
THIS IS HOW WE'LL BRING DOWN THE NAZI THREAT FROM THE SKY. YOU HAVE ORDERS TO SHOOT DOWN EVERY ENEMY FIGHTER PLANE YOU CATCH SIGHT OF.

MARX SPOKE HIGHLY OF LIEUTENANT BLECKER.
HONOR THE MOTHERLAND AND WIN THIS WAR!

PROBABLY BECAUSE HE WAS ONE OF THE ONLY OFFICERS HE KNEW THAT WAS JEWISH.

MARX MOSEIVICH! MARX MOSEIVICH!

KEEP IT DOWN! WHAT THE HELL IS GOING ON?!
I'M REPORTING FOR DUTY, SIR!

SIR?
WHEN MARX FIRST CAME TO MILITARY SCHOOL, EVERYONE WAS REPORTING TO STEPAN.
TWO WEEKS LATER, STEPAN RECEIVED ORDERS TO REPORT TO MARX.

ALL RIGHT, LOAD UP THE TRUCK. WE'RE MOVING OUT IN 0400.
YES, SIR!

BY THE WAY, YOU'RE DRIVING.

MARX FIGURED THAT IF STEPAN DROVE HE'D TALK LESS.

SO I TOLD HIM TO GO *FUCK* HIMSELF AND I MARRIED HIS DAUGHTER. SHE IS A GOOD *FUCKING* WOMAN.
HE WAS WRONG. STEPAN TALKED EVEN MORE WHEN HE DROVE.

MARX HATED WHEN PEOPLE TALKED TOO MUCH.
ESPECIALLY MY GRANDMOTHER.
AND SO I TELL HER THIS DRESS NOT COMPLIMENT HER FIGURE AND SHE SAY ME SHE JUST LOSE WEIGHT. *BULL SHIT!* SHE IS STILL FAT COW!
OY VEY!

WHAT YOU WANT, MARX? I AM ON PHONE!
WITH BORIS YELTSIN? YOU NOT TALKING ANYTHING IMPORTANT. *HANG UP PHONE AND SHUT UP!*

WHY YOU CARE IF I TALK ON PHONE? *YOU SHUT UP!*
HMPH!

ONRISHINKA HAS COME!
MY GRANDFATHER HAD BEEN IN THE HOSPITAL FOR THREE DAYS. I CAME TO VISIT HIM EVERY EVENING IN ORDER TO HELP BOOST HIS MORALE.

YOU'RE BURNING UP.
IT'S OKAY! IT'S OKAY! DOCTOR SAY EVERYTHING FINE. SURGERY WAS SUCCESS. I GO HOME SOON.

YOU DON'T LOOK GOOD. I'M GOING TO GET THE NURSE.
IT'S OKAY. SIT DOWN. I'M OKAY.

EXCUSE ME?
I CAN'T WAIT TO GET OUT OF HERE AND TAKE A NICE WARM BATH.
DON'T FORGET TO PUT SOME CUCUMBER SLICES OVER YOUR EYES. IT'S *A-MAZING!*
AH-*HEM.*

CAN I HELP YOU?
UHM, SOMETHING'S WRONG WITH MY GRANDFATHER. HE'S COME DOWN WITH A BAD FEVER ALL OF A SUDDEN.
OH DON'T WORRY ABOUT IT. HIS FEVER WILL GO DOWN IN A BIT. THANKS.

SIT. I WANT TELL YOU SOMETHING.
FOR THIS BOOK ABOUT ME YOU WRITE.

I REMEMBER FIRST THING I SEE WHEN WAR START.

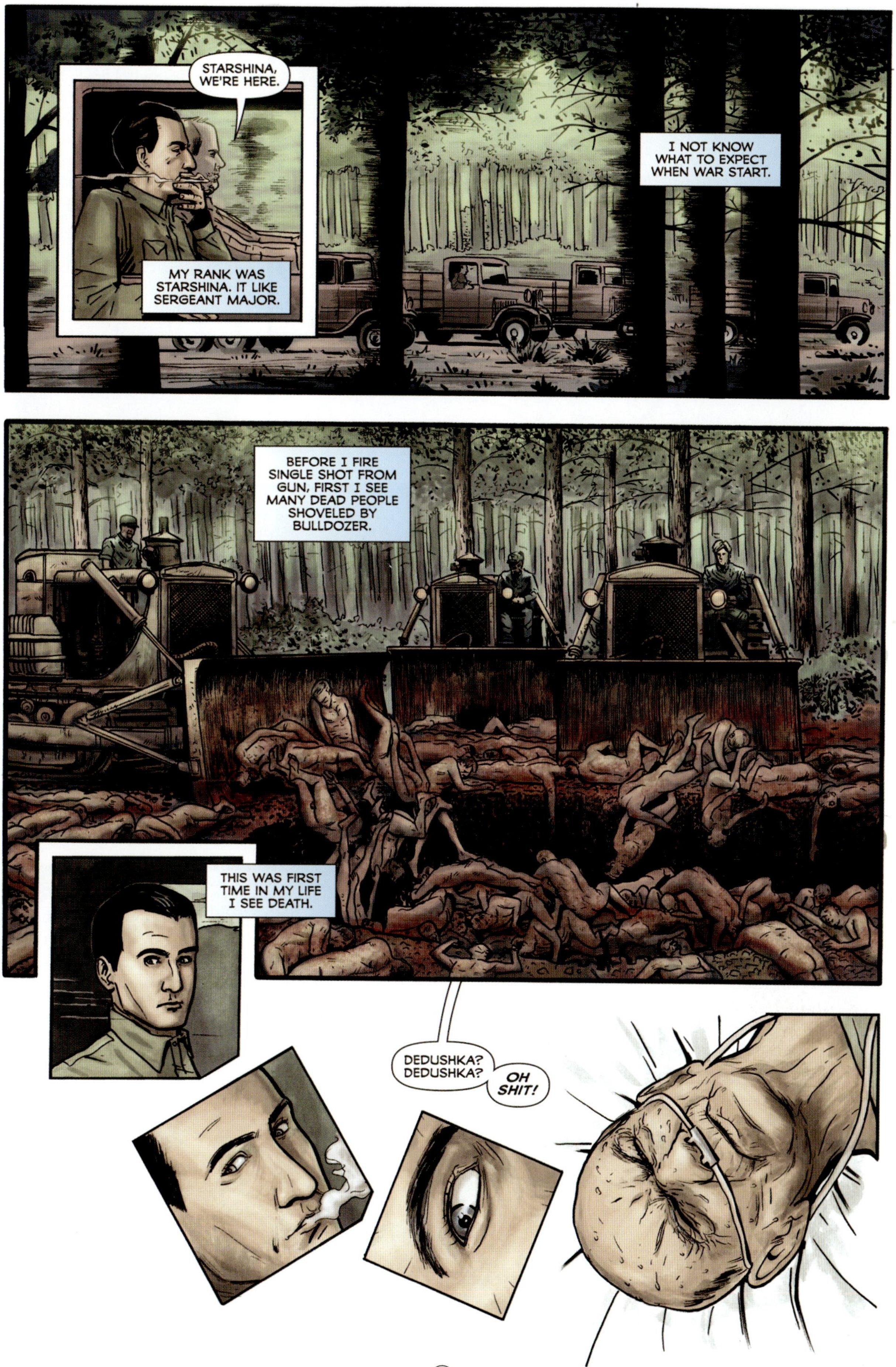

BEFORE I FIRE SINGLE SHOT FROM GUN, FIRST I SEE MANY DEAD PEOPLE SHOVELED BY BULLDOZER.

THIS WAS FIRST TIME IN MY LIFE I SEE DEATH.

DEDUSHKA? DEDUSHKA?

OH SHIT!

WHAT'S GOING ON?
WE NEED TO MOVE YOUR GRANDFATHER TO THE ICU NOW!

HE'S LOST A LOT OF BLOOD AND IF WE DON'T STABILIZE HIM, WE'LL HAVE TO BRING HIM BACK TO SURGERY.

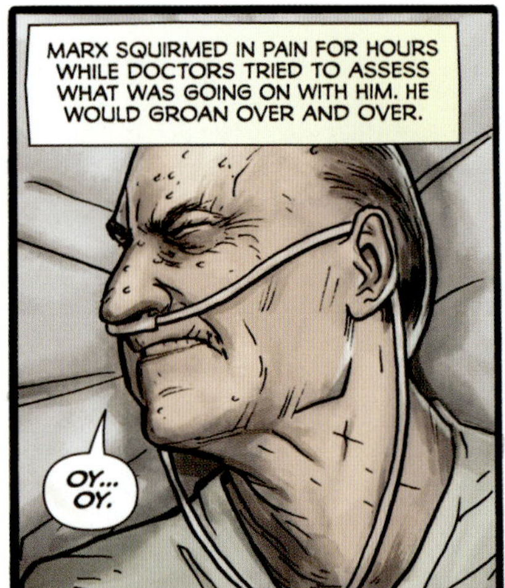
MARX SQUIRMED IN PAIN FOR HOURS WHILE DOCTORS TRIED TO ASSESS WHAT WAS GOING ON WITH HIM. HE WOULD GROAN OVER AND OVER.
OY... OY.

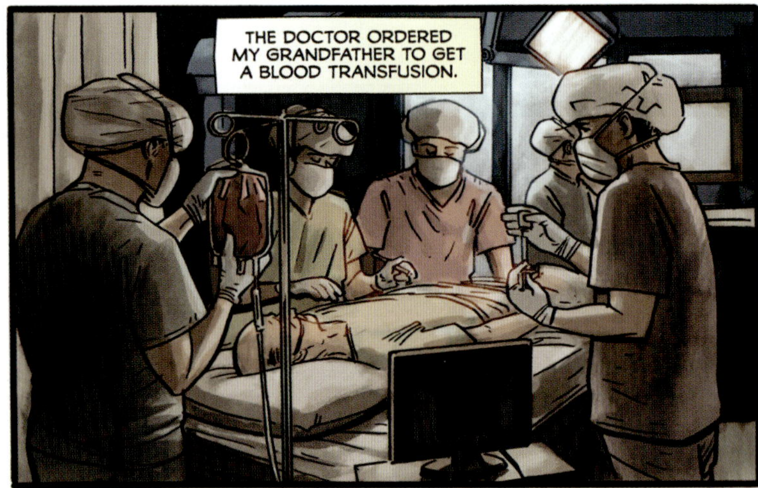
THE DOCTOR ORDERED MY GRANDFATHER TO GET A BLOOD TRANSFUSION.

HE NOT NEED BLOOD! SURGEON DID NOT CLOSE INCISION PROPERLY!

MA'AM, WE ARE DOING EVERYTHING WE CAN. WE'RE JUST STARTING OFF BY FOLLOWING A FEW STANDARD PROCEDURES.
YOU NEED TO USE YOUR BRAIN! HE IS HEALTHY MAN! YOU KILLING HIM! HE NEED SURGERY!

SEEING HIM IN SUCH PAIN MADE ME WANT TO LEAVE THE HOSPITAL, BUT I COULDN'T--SO I IGNORED EVERYTHING THAT WAS GOING ON AROUND ME.
I BEGAN LISTENING TO AN INTERVIEW I DID WITH MARX WHERE HE TOLD ME ABOUT HIS FIRST ACT OF VALOR DURING THE WAR.
MARX'S UNIT WAS UNDER HEAVY FIRE. THE SOVIETS WERE UNDER ATTACK FROM ALL DIRECTIONS.
AND TO MAKE MATTERS WORSE, THEY LOST A CRATE FULL OF AMMUNITION.

WHERE'S THE AMMUNITION?
THE CRATE FELL OFF THE BACK OF THE TRUCK.

GODDAMN IT! WHERE'S BIARSKY?
WE HAVEN'T SEEN HIM, SIR.

THE AMMO CASE WAS ABOUT 100 YARDS AHEAD OF THEIR POSITION AND IT WEIGHED 200 POUNDS.
YOU TWO. YOU'RE COMING WITH ME!
WHERE ARE WE GOING?

TO GET THAT AMMO!
NOT ONLY DID MARX RUN THE LENGTH OF A FOOTBALL FIELD TO FETCH A 200 POUND CRATE OF AMMUNITION...

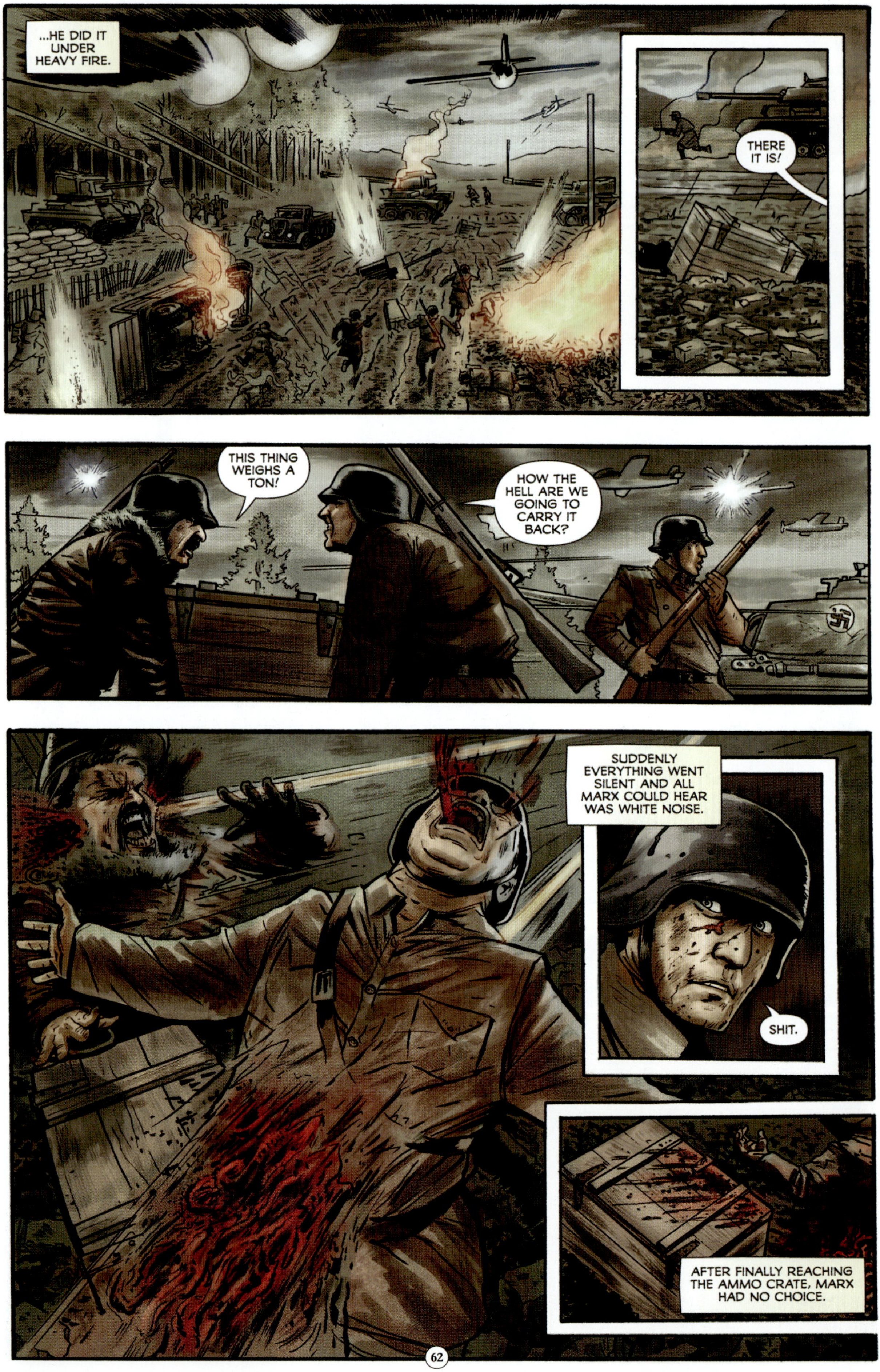

SUDDENLY EVERYTHING WENT SILENT AND ALL MARX COULD HEAR WAS WHITE NOISE.

SHIT.

AFTER FINALLY REACHING THE AMMO CRATE, MARX HAD NO CHOICE.

HE RAN BACK TO HIS UNIT WITH A 200-POUND CRATE OF AMMUNITION OVER HIS SHOULDERS....
...WITH A NAZI PLANE SHOOTING AT HIM THE WHOLE TIME.

LOAD UP THE GAZ AND SHOOT DOWN THAT PLANE!
YES, STARSHINA!

I FOUND IT HARD TO BELIEVE AT FIRST.

BUT SEEING HOW MANY TIMES MY GRANDFATHER OVERCAME OVERWHELMING ODDS IN THE HOSPITAL MADE A BELIEVER OUT OF ME.
I THINK THAT THE FEAR AND PRESSURE OF STARING DEATH IN THE FACE GAVE HIM THE ABILITY TO PERFORM THIS INCREDIBLE FEAT.

MY GRANDFATHER WAS NOT A VICTIM OF NAZI GERMANY.

HE WAS A FIGHTER.

BUT MORE THAN THAT...

MARX!
MARX!
MARX!
...HE WAS A LEADER.

A COUPLE OF HOURS AFTER MARX WAS BROUGHT INTO THE ICU, THE DOCTOR FINALLY CAME TO CHECK BACK ON US.
LOOK, FOR THE LAST HOUR, WE'VE HAD NURSES COMING IN AND OUT OF OUR ROOM ASKING THE SAME QUESTIONS OVER AND OVER AGAIN. WHAT'S GOING ON?
WE NEED TO TAKE YOUR GRANDFATHER BACK TO SURGERY. THE SURGEONS DIDN'T PROPERLY SEAL HIS INCISION.

WE CAN'T OPERATE ON YOUR GRANDFATHER UNLESS YOU SIGN THIS FORM. IT BASICALLY PROTECTS THE HOSPITAL FROM BEING HELD LIABLE IN CASE SOMETHING HAPPENS.
AND JUST LIKE THAT, MY GRANDFATHER'S LIFE WAS PLACED IN MY HANDS.

I SIGNED HIS LIFE AWAY. IT WAS EITHER THAT OR WATCH HIM DIE.

TWO HOURS LATER, A NURSE ENTERED THE WAITING ROOM.
IS EVERYTHING OKAY?
OH, I HAVE NO IDEA. I WAS JUST ASKED TO BRING THIS TO YOU.
IT WAS AS IF NOBODY CARED OR HAD ANY SYMPATHY FOR WHAT MY FAMILY WAS GOING THROUGH.
WE HAD NO IDEA IF MARX WAS DEAD OR ALIVE.

MARX ONCE WROTE A STORY ABOUT ONE OF HIS EXPERIENCES DURING THE WAR.
IT WAS THE STORY OF HOW HE ALMOST DIED ON NEW YEARS EVE, 1941.
I *FUCKING* HATE WALKING ON ICE. I WANT *FUCKING* VODKA.
NEW YEARS IS THE MOST CELEBRATED HOLIDAY IN RUSSIA. COME HELL OR HIGH WATER, RUSSIANS ARE GOING TO FIND A WAY TO GET SHIT FACED. WAR OR NO WAR.

THE SOVIET MILITARY MANAGED TO KEEP THE NAZIS FROM TAKING MOSCOW. THEY PUSHED THEM BACK TO THE WESTERN FRONT AND NOW THE WAR HAD REACHED A TEMPORARY STALEMATE.
YOU AND ME BOTH. WALK FASTER. WE'RE ALMOST THERE.
DO YOU HEAR THAT NOISE?

THERE HADN'T BEEN ANY ACTION IN WEEKS.
STARSHINA! GET DOWN!

BADOOM!

OH *FUCK.*
THE NAZIS WAGED WAR ON THE ONE NIGHT THEY KNEW THEIR ENEMY WOULD BE MOST VULNERABLE.

FUCK!
FUCK!
FUCK!

I'VE GOT YOU!

WE'RE ALMOST AT THE CAMP!

WE MADE IT!
DON'T WORRY STARSHINA, I'LL BE RIGHT BACK!

HE'S MY COMMANDING OFFICER! WE NEED TO FUCKING GET HIM OUT OF HERE!

YOU GOT HIM?
YEAH. ON MY COUNT. ONE--TWO--*THREE!*
MARX WAS VERY CLEAR IN HIS STORY THAT IF IT WASN'T FOR STEPAN, HE WOULD HAVE DIED.
MARX SURVIVED SURGERY AFTER SURGERY IN HIS LATER YEARS THE SAME WAY HE SURVIVED BATTLE AFTER BATTLE ON THE FRONT LINES IN HIS YOUTH.

GET HIM OUT OF HERE. HE OUTRANKS EVERYONE ELSE.

YOU'RE GOING TO BE ALL RIGHT, COMRADE!

HE DIDN'T SKIMP ON ANY DETAILS IN HIS STORY. FOR A MAN WHO ENJOYED GLOATING, THIS WAS DEFINITELY NOT HIS PROUDEST MOMENT.
HE DIDN'T KILL ANY NAZIS THAT NIGHT OR LIBERATE ANY JEWS FROM CONCENTRATION CAMPS.
ALL HE MANAGED TO DO WAS SURVIVE THE ICE-COLD HELL STORM THAT ERUPTED ON THE ZHIZDRA RIVER.

THE OPERATION WAS A SUCCESS. YOUR GRANDFATHER IS GOING TO BE ALL RIGHT.

THANK YOU, DOCTOR. WE APPRECIATE EVERYTHING YOU'VE DONE FOR US TONIGHT.
IT'S MY PLEASURE.

NEXT TIME YOU WILL LISTEN TO ME.

YES, WE SURE WILL.

IDIOT!

WE WERE LUCKY THAT NIGHT.

ON MY WAY OUT OF THE HOSPITAL, I SAW A FAMILY THAT WAS IN THE ICU ROOM NEXT TO MARX.

I'M SORRY--BUT YOUR FATHER DIDN'T MAKE IT.
THAT COULD HAVE BEEN ME AND MY GRANDMOTHER.

AS I APPROACHED THE ELEVATOR, I COULD HEAR THE FAINT ECHO OF THAT FAMILY CRYING IN UNISON.

THEY WOULD NEVER SEE THEIR LOVED ONE AGAIN.

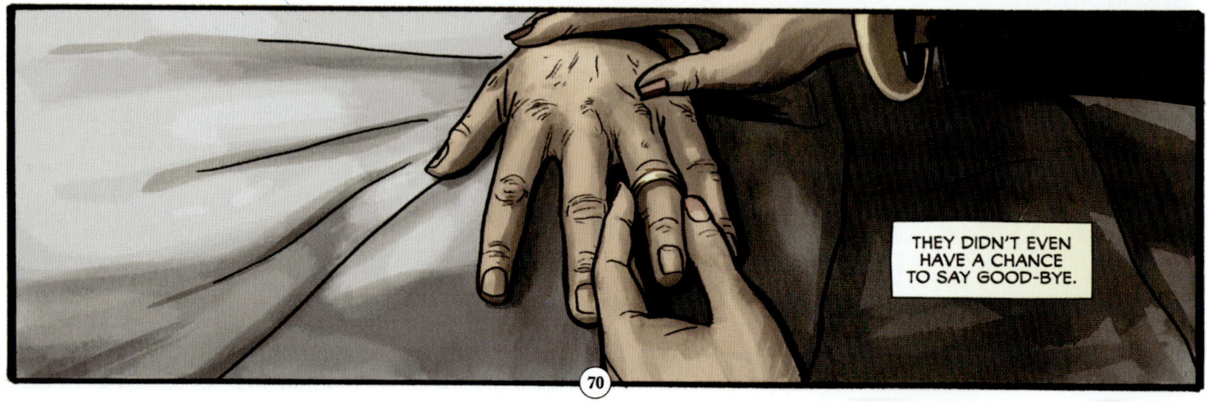
THEY DIDN'T EVEN HAVE A CHANCE TO SAY GOOD-BYE.

WHEN I
CAME HOME
I COULDN'T
FALL SLEEP.
EVEN THOUGH HE WAS
OKAY, I KNEW THAT IT
WOULD ONLY BE A
MATTER OF TIME
BEFORE MARX ENDED
UP BACK IN THE ICU.
IN THAT MOMENT,
I FELT LUCKY THAT
I DIDN'T HAVE TO
DEAL WITH WHAT
THAT FAMILY WAS
DEALING WITH.

IT COULD HAVE
BEEN THAT WAY. MARX
COULD HAVE DIED AND
I WOULD HAVE BEEN THE
ONE STANDING THERE
CONSOLING MY
GRANDMOTHER.
THANK GOD IT
WASN'T SO.

AT LEAST
NOT YET.

NO MATTER HOW HARD HE FOUGHT, ALL OF HIS VICTORIES WERE SHORT-LIVED.

ППГ655

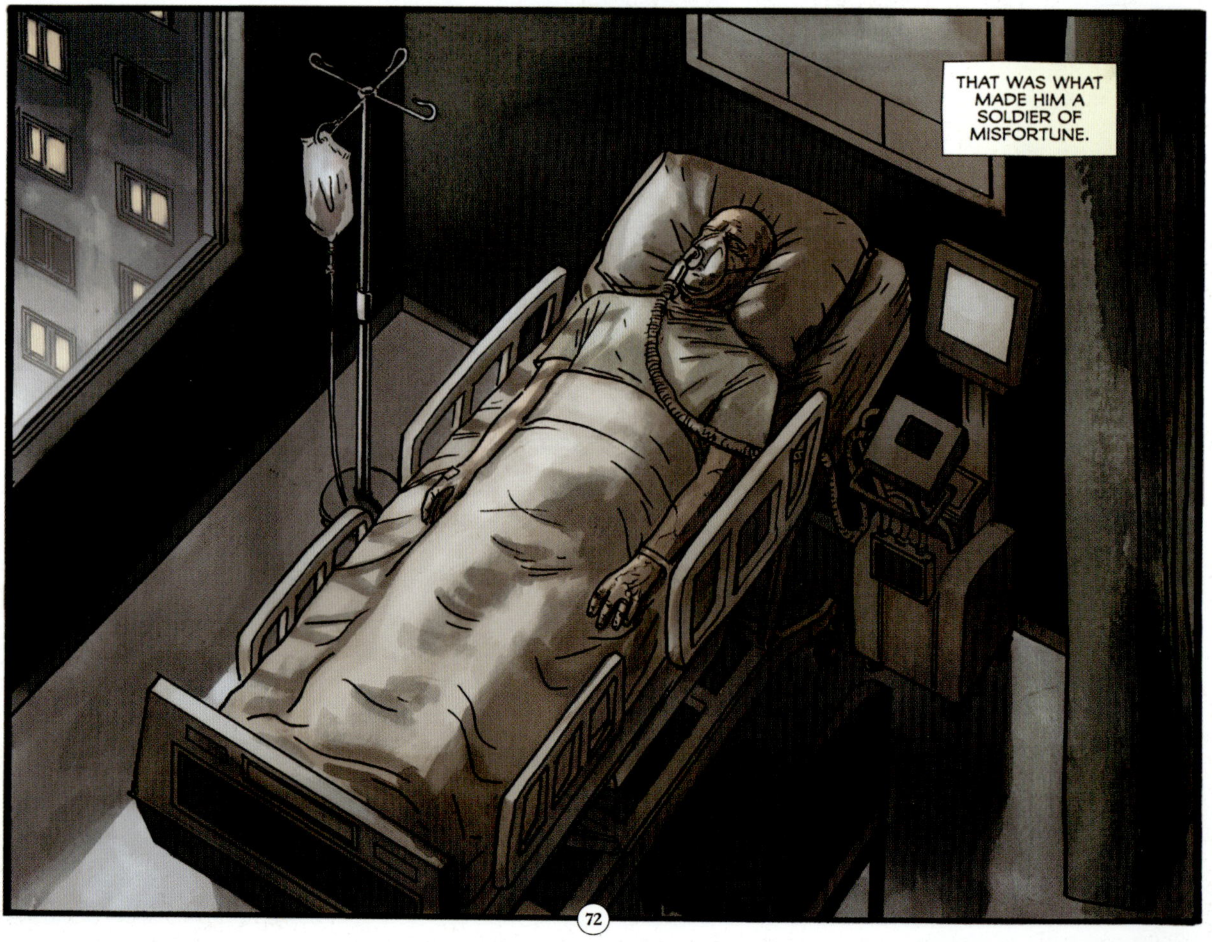

THAT WAS WHAT MADE HIM A SOLDIER OF MISFORTUNE.

CHAPTER 4:

ENEMY OF THE STATE

Onrie Kompan
WRITER

Dan Dougherty
ARTIST

Kanila Tripp
COLORIST

Ed Dukeshire
LETTERER

JM DeMatteis
EDITOR

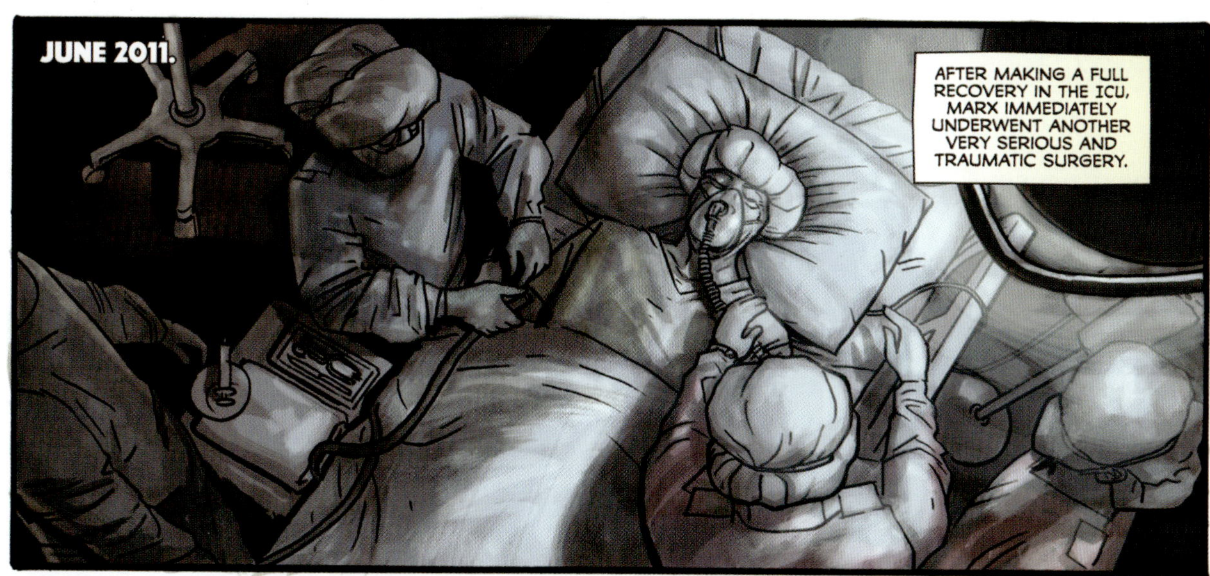
JUNE 2011.
AFTER MAKING A FULL RECOVERY IN THE ICU, MARX IMMEDIATELY UNDERWENT ANOTHER VERY SERIOUS AND TRAUMATIC SURGERY.

HE SURVIVED.
A FEW NIGHTS LATER, HE GOT UP FROM HIS HOSPITAL BED AND STARTED MAKING HIS WAY FOR THE EXIT.

AFTER TAKING JUST A FEW STEPS, HE HIT THE GROUND HARD-- CHIPPING A BONE IN HIS HIP.

HE WOULDN'T WALK AGAIN AFTER THAT.

SOON AFTER, HE BEGAN TO DEVELOP NASTY BED SORES.
THE BOTTOMS OF HIS FEET WERE ALL SCARRED.

JULY 2011.
THE HOSPITAL COULDN'T DO ANYTHING FOR MARX AND SO THEY EVENTUALLY MOVED HIM TO A REHABILITATION CENTER.

HE HATED IT THERE. HIS PHYSICAL THERAPIST HAD GIVEN UP ON HIM AND I HAD TO ADMIT THAT EVEN I BECAME FRUSTRATED WITH MY GRANDFATHER. I'D NEVER SEEN HIM LIKE THIS BEFORE.
IF YOU DON'T GET OUT OF BED, YOU'LL NEVER GO HOME! DON'T YOU GET THAT?!
I UNDERSTAND.
THEN STAND UP!
I CAN'T!

NO MATTER HOW HARD HE FOUGHT TO RECUPERATE, HE JUST KEPT FAILING. SO HE STOPPED TRYING AND ACCEPTED THAT THIS WAS HIS END.
THERE WAS NOTHING WE COULD DO TO SAVE HIM FROM HIMSELF.

AUGUST 2011.
A MONTH LATER, THE REHAB CENTER RELEASED MARX AND HE FINALLY CAME HOME AFTER THREE MONTHS OF BEING AWAY.

HE WANTED TO COME HOME SO BADLY. BUT EVEN THOUGH HE FINALLY GOT WHAT HE WANTED, HE WASN'T THE SAME ANY MORE.

AUGUST 2ND, 2011.
GRANDPA, I HAVE SOME QUESTIONS FOR YOU. IT'S FOR MY STORY.
SIT. I TELL YOU EVERYTHING.
MY GRANDFATHER'S TIME ON EARTH WAS RUNNING OUT. THIS WAS MY LAST CHANCE TO GET HIS STORY AND MY FINAL INTERVIEW WITH HIM.

AS HE LAY IN BED DYING, I FOUND IT SO HARD TO BELIEVE.
BOOM!
...THAT A MAN WHO SURVIVED A WAR THAT CLAIMED THE LIVES OF MILLIONS....
BOOM!
RUSSIA, 1942.
...COULD BECOME HIS OWN WORST ENEMY.
BOOM!

AFTER NEARLY DYING ON NEW YEARS EVE 1941, MARX WOKE UP TWO DAYS LATER IN AN INFIRMARY THAT WAS UNDER ATTACK BY THE NAZIS.
AM I BLIND? *I'M BLIND!*

HE HAD NO IDEA HOW HE GOT THERE.
NOT BLIND.

ALL HE KNEW WAS THAT IF HE STAYED IN THAT INFIRMARY FOR A SECOND LONGER, HE WOULD DIE.

HE HADN'T EVEN FULLY RECOVERED YET.

BUT HE HAD NO CHOICE.

HIS ONLY OPTION WAS TO FIGHT AND LIVE...

...OR TO STAY AND DIE.

IN ORDER TO SURVIVE, MARX HAD TO KEEP HIS MIND STRONG.

MARX FUCKING MOSEIVICH! YOU'RE ALIVE!

READY FOR BATTLE, SIR?

BOYS, LET'S GET STARSHINA MELNIK SOME HOT FUCKING TEA.
HE LOOKS LIKE HELL, SIR. MAYBE HE SHOULD LIE DOWN?
BULLSHIT! HE LOOKS FINE AS FUCK!
NOW HURRY THE FUCK UP!

THE NEXT DAY, MARX WAS BACK ON THE FRONTLINES.

DID YOU HEAR THAT?
WHAT?

I ASKED MARX IF HE HAD EVER KILLED ANYONE.

HE SHRUGGED HIS SHOULDERS AND SAID...
"I DON'T KNOW.

"WHEN NAZI SHOOT AT ME, I SHOOT AT THEM.

"I NOT KNOW IF I KILL ANYONE.

"I NOT CARE IF I KILL ANYONE.

"I JUST DO MY JOB."

HOLD YOUR FIRE!

STARSHINA?

YOUR LEG IS BLEEDING.

HMPH!
I'M ALL RIGHT. IT DIDN'T GO IN DEEP. LET'S MOVE.
SIR, WE SHOULD BANDAGE THAT UP RIGHT AWAY.
LATER.

THERE WAS TOO MUCH DISTANCE BETWEEN MARX AND THE ENEMY FOR HIM TO EVER KNOW FOR SURE IF HE HAD KILLED ANYONE.

BUT THAT DIDN'T MATTER. HE KEPT FIRING UNTIL EVERYTHING WENT DEAD SILENT.
HE NEVER BRAGGED ABOUT KILLING NAZIS. HE JUST SAID IT WAS A JOB THAT NEEDED TO BE DONE.

THIS WAS THE ONLY WAY TO JUSTIFY THE ACT OF KILLING AND TO MAKE SENSE OF THE HELL HE WITNESSED ON THE FRONTLINES.
...WHAT THE HELL IS GOING ON OUT HERE?! THE NAZIS ARE KICKING OUR ASSES!
YOU ALL LACK THE PROPER MOTIVATION.
MARX ALWAYS SAID THAT WAR WAS A JOB. IT WAS NO DIFFERENT TO HIM THAN WORKING IN A FACTORY.

PERHAPS THAT WAS HIS WAY OF MAKING SENSE OF ALL THE CHAOS.

IN MY HAND IS THE ORDER OF LENIN. THERE IS NO MEDAL MORE PRESTIGIOUS!
EVERY SOLDIER THAT SHOOTS DOWN A NAZI PLANE WILL BE AWARDED ONE ORDER OF LENIN MEDAL.

THE ORDER OF LENIN WAS RESERVED FOR CITIZENS OF THE SOVIET UNION THAT HAD ACHIEVED SOMETHING TRULY SIGNIFICANT. BEFORE THE WAR, ONLY 100 MEN WERE GIVEN THIS MEDAL.

MARX COULD CARE LESS ABOUT THE MEDALS. HE WAS GIVEN DOZENS OF THEM WHILE HE SERVED ON THE FRONTLINES.
MELNIK. BIARSKY. I WANT A WORD.
MOSES MELNIK WAS ONE OF THE ORIGINAL RECIPIENTS.

TOMORROW MORNING AT 0600, THERE WILL BE A SOVIET PLANE HEADING TOWARDS MOSCOW. YOU'LL KNOW IT'S A FRIENDLY BECAUSE A GREEN LIGHT WILL BE SHINING FROM UNDERNEATH IT.
MAKE SURE YOUR MEN DON'T SHOOT DOWN THAT PLANE.
YES SIR!

THE NEXT MORNING. 0600.

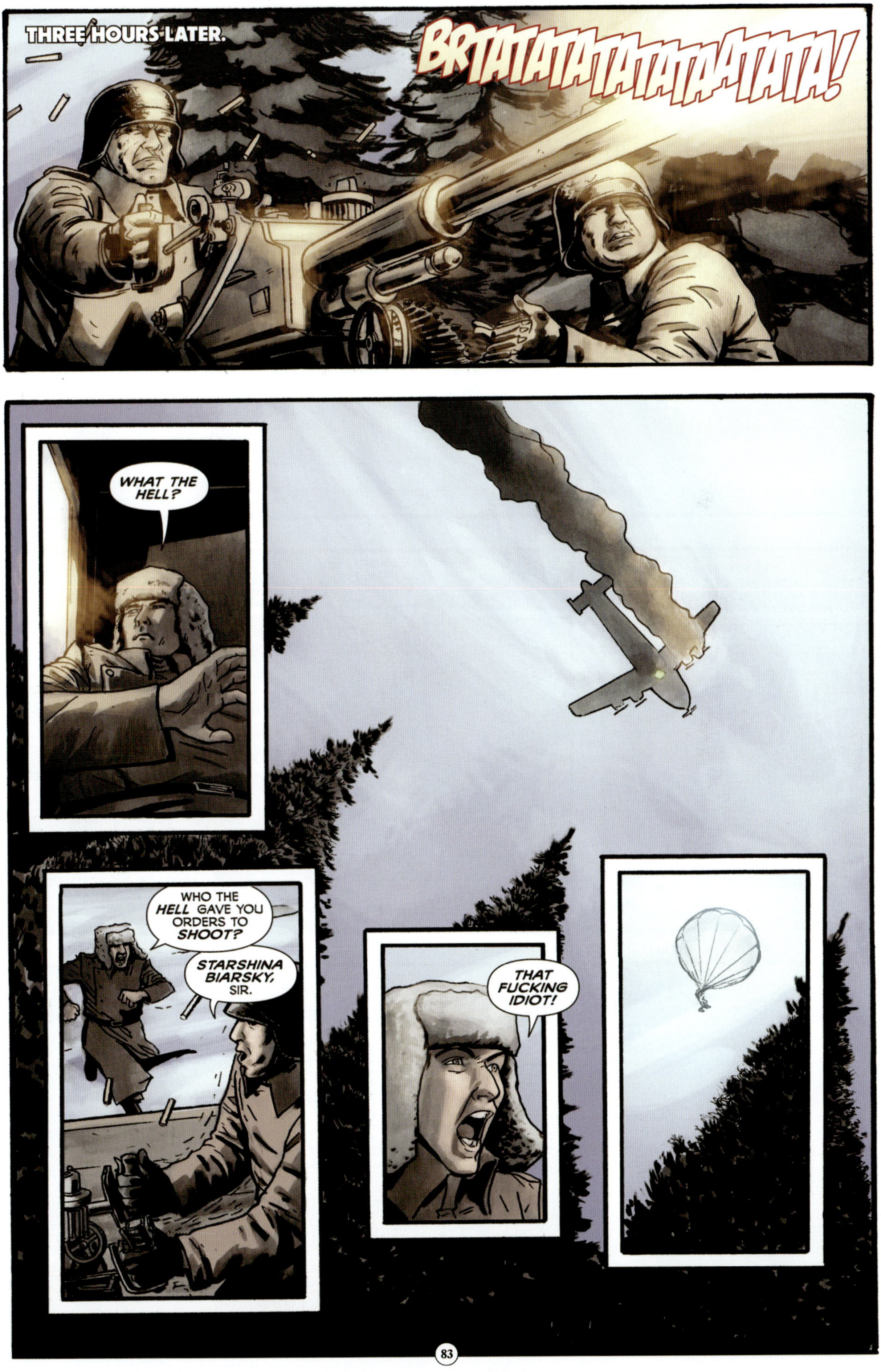

WHAT THE HELL?

WHO THE *HELL* GAVE YOU ORDERS TO *SHOOT*?

STARSHINA BIARSKY, SIR.

THAT FUCKING IDIOT!

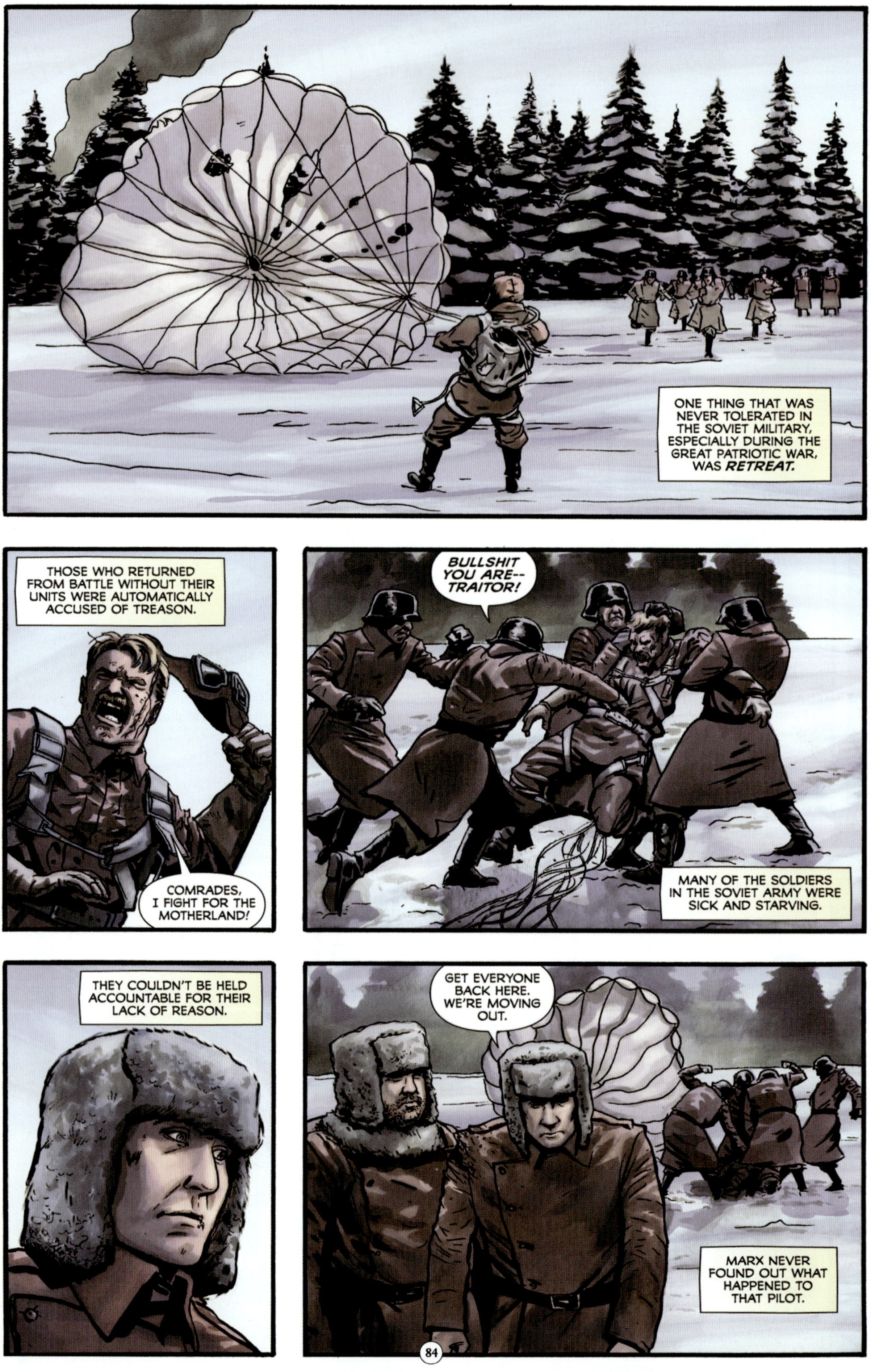

ONE THING THAT WAS NEVER TOLERATED IN THE SOVIET MILITARY, ESPECIALLY DURING THE GREAT PATRIOTIC WAR, WAS ***RETREAT.***

MARX WAS STRUGGLING A LOT DURING THE FIRST PART OF THE INTERVIEW. WORDS WEREN'T COMING TO HIM VERY EASILY AND THAT FRUSTRATED HIM.

AND THEN HE LOOKED OVER AT ME AND SAID.
I KNOW WHAT IS LIKE TO BE IN LABOR.
LIKE WOMAN.

DURING WAR, MY MEN AND I FIGHTING FOR DAYS. SOMETIMES WE EAT. SOMETIMES NOT.

ONE DAY, WE COME TO SMALL VILLAGE.

MY MEN AND I ARE TIRED. IS IT OKAY IF WE CAN REST HERE?
OF COURSE, SINOCHIK!
DO YOU HAVE ANYTHING FOR US TO EAT OR TO DRINK?

NOT A MORSEL OF FOOD NOR A DROP OF WATER.

FUCK.
RELAX. AT LEAST WE CAN FINALLY SLEEP WITH A ROOF OVER OUR HEADS TONIGHT.

THE NAZIS CAME HERE AND TOOK EVERYTHING FROM US. WE BARELY HAVE ENOUGH CLOTHES TO PUT ON OUR BACKS.

STARSHINA! COME HERE QUICK!

AND BRING THAT FUCKING BABA WITH YOU!

SEEMS LIKE THE NAZIS DIDN'T TAKE EVERYTHING.

STEPAN, SEE IF YOU CAN FIND US SOMETHING TO DRINK.
WE DON'T HAVE VODKA HERE!
FUCK YES SIR!

MY MEN HAVEN'T EATEN IN DAYS AND HAVE SEEN ENOUGH ACTION TO LAST TWO LIFETIMES! IF WE FIND VODKA, WE'RE DRINKING EVERY LAST DROP!

STARSHINA! I *FUCKING* FOUND SOMETHING!

I DON'T THINK IT'S VODKA, BUT IT'LL DEFINITELY GET US DRUNK.
IT'S GOOD ENOUGH. GET SOME GLASSES FOR THE OTHER MEN.

ALL SOLDIER TAKE ONE SHOT.

BUT I DRINK *ONE CUP!*
WHY A FULL CUP?

BECAUSE I STRONGER THAN ALL OF THEM!

DID YOU GET DRUNK?
NO. I NOT GET DRUNK. IT WAS NOT ALCOHOL.
THEN WHAT THE HELL WAS IT?

EARLY NEXT MORNING I WAKE UP IN GREAT PAIN.

MY STOMACH HURTING SO BAD, I FEEL LIKE I ABOUT TO HAVE BABY!

STEPAN, *GET THAT BABA OVER HERE NOW!*
FUCK... YES...SIR!

WHAT THE HELL DID YOU GIVE US, BABUSHKA?
I KEPT TELLING THIS BIG BUFFOON THAT THE BOTTLE HE TOOK WAS NOT ALCOHOL. IT'S WHAT WE GIVE TO WOMEN WHEN THEY ARE DELIVERING BABIES!

YOU'RE A GOD DAMN MORON, STEPAN!
HE HAD GIVEN EVERYONE, INCLUDING MARX, THE EQUIVALENT OF OXYTOCIN,

I'M FUCKING SORRY, SIR.

SO MARX CLAIMED THAT HE KNEW WHAT IT WAS LIKE TO BE IN LABOR. I'M NOT SURE IF THE PAIN HE FELT COULD ACTUALLY COMPARE, BUT, EITHER WAY, THAT WAS A PRETTY SHITTY SITUATION.

WHEN MARX HAD DOWNTIME, HE WOULD READ AND EXCHANGE LETTERS WITH *ELENA SABOTSKIYA,* HIS FRIEND FROM HIGH SCHOOL, WHO WAS ALSO FIGHTING ON THE FRONTLINES.

ELENA WAS DROPPING BOMBS FROM AIRPLANES AND WAS CONSTANTLY FLYING TO AND FROM GERMANY.
YET SHE STILL WENT OUT OF HER WAY TO STAY IN TOUCH WITH MARX.
AND BECAUSE HE HAD NO ONE ELSE, HE DID THE SAME.

THEY COMMUNICATED IN *CODE* SO THAT NO ONE WOULD BE ABLE TO UNDERSTAND THE MESSAGES THAT THEY WROTE TO EACH OTHER.
MARX ALWAYS RESPECTED ELENA. SHE WAS A VERY SMART WOMAN AND HE WAS ABLE TO RELATE TO HER ON AN *INTELLECTUAL LEVEL.*

MELNIK!
RIGHT HERE!

I ONCE ASKED MARX IF THERE WAS ANYTHING HE WAS AFRAID OF DURING THE WAR.

I WAS SCARE OF NOTHING! IF I DIE, I GO TO BE WITH PARENTS IN HEAVEN.

WHENEVER I ASKED HIM WHAT HIS THOUGHTS WERE ABOUT STALIN, HE WOULD SCOFF AND SAY--
HE IS MAFIOSNIK! THEY ALL WERE GOONS. STALIN. HITLER. ALL SAME. CRIMINAL!

AND THAT WOULD LEAD HIM INTO A RANT.
ALL YOU KIDS TODAY ARE SPOIL! YOU NOT UNDERSTAND ANYTHING!
WHEN I WAS BOY, EDUCATION WAS EVERYTHING. TODAY IS ALWAYS MONEY, MONEY MONEY! BECAUSE OF PEOPLE LIKE THEM!

DO YOU BELIEVE IN COMMUNISM?
YES. I AM REAL COMMUNIST.

COMMUNISM IS HELPING OTHER PEOPLE. EDUCATING OTHER PEOPLE. TODAY, NO ONE CARING ABOUT EDUCATION.

BECAUSE STALIN KILL EVERYONE WITH EDUCATION.

SO MANY PEOPLE DIED DURING WORLD WAR II THAT IT WAS IMPOSSIBLE TO KEEP TRACK OF JUST HOW MANY LIVES WERE LOST.
MANY HISTORIANS BELIEVE THAT STALIN'S BODY COUNT FAR SURPASSED HITLER'S.
THE SOVIET UNION WAS NOTORIOUS FOR MAKING PEOPLE DISAPPEAR ON AND OFF THE BATTLEFIELD BEFORE, AND ESPECIALLY DURING, THE WAR.
THEY LOOKED FOR ANY EXCUSE THEY COULD TO THROW PEOPLE IN JAIL OR WORSE HAVE THEM EXECUTED.
NO REMORSE WAS GIVEN, ESPECIALLY TO SOLDIERS WHO TURNED THEIR BACKS TO THE ENEMY.

MARX MADE A CRAZY CLAIM DURING THAT LAST INTERVIEW. HE SAID THAT BEFORE THE WAR ENDED, HE WAS A COLONEL IN THE RUSSIAN MILITARY.
WHEN I TOLD THIS TO MY FATHER, HE CHUCKLED AND TOLD ME THAT THIS WAS IMPOSSIBLE.

HE WAS RIGHT. MARX WAS ONLY 24 YEARS OLD WHEN THE WAR ENDED. THERE WAS NO WAY HE COULD HAVE BEEN A COLONEL.

AND THEN I ASKED MY GRANDMOTHER AND FOUND OUT THE TRUTH.
YOUR GRANDFATHER FIGHT IN WAR FOR ONLY ONE AND A HALF YEARS.

WAIT. HE SAID HE FOUGHT THROUGHOUT THE WAR.

NO. HE WAS SENT TO GULAG.
GU--WHAT?

GULAG. IS WORSE THAN PRISON!
BUT WHY WOULD ANYONE HAVE WANTED TO ARREST HIM?

MELNIK!
HERE!
"BECAUSE STALIN SAY HE WAS *ENEMY OF THE STATE.*"

I EVENTUALLY DISCOVERED THAT MARX WASN'T LYING.

HE WAS LIED *TO.*
STARSHINA, FOR YOUR NOBLE EFFORTS IN SERVING MOTHER RUSSIA, COMRADE STALIN HAS PROMOTED YOU TO THE RANK OF *COLONEL.*
YOU HAVE ORDERS TO COME BACK TO MOSCOW WITH US.

I'LL GET MY THINGS.
THERE IS *NO TIME,* COMRADE. SAY GOODBYE TO YOUR MEN.

STARSHINA? WHERE ARE YOU GOING?
YOU'RE IN CHARGE OF THE MEN NOW, STEPAN. I HAVE NEW ORDERS.

THERE ARE MANY STORIES OF PEOPLE THAT SUDDENLY DISAPPEARED FROM THE FRONT LINES.

IT COULD HAPPEN AT ANY MOMENT. WHEN YOU LEAST EXPECTED IT.

THE NKVD WAS A WELL OILED MACHINE. THEY FOOLED MARX INTO THINKING THAT HE WAS OFF TO BIGGER AND BETTER THINGS.
UNF!
I WILL FUCKING MISS YOU, SIR!

THEY MADE HIM FEEL LIKE HE WAS ON TOP OF THE WORLD.
GOODBYE.

LIKE HE MATTERED.

LIKE HE WAS A PART OF SOMETHING.

AND THEN JUST LIKE THAT--
THEY TOOK IT ALL AWAY.

MARX MOSEIVICH MELNIK, YOU ARE UNDER ARREST FOR TREASON AGAINST MOTHER RUSSIA.
WHAT THE HELL ARE YOU TALKING ABOUT? WHERE ARE YOU TAKING ME?

LEFORTOVO.

HE WASN'T AN ENEMY OF THE STATE.

HE WAS THE UNFORTUNATE VICTIM OF BRUTAL TIMES AND HARSH CIRCUMSTANCES.

CHAPTER 5:
WORKER'S PARADISE

Onrie Kompan
WRITER

Vassilis Gogtzilas
ARTIST

Nick Bell
COLORIST

Ed Dukeshire
LETTERER

JM DeMatteis
EDITOR

I REMEMBER SEEING MARX'S LIFELESS BODY ON THE NIGHT OF HIS PASSING. IT WAS ONE OF THE MOST SAD AND PROFOUND MOMENTS OF MY LIFE.
HE LOOKED LIKE A WAX FIGURE WITH A LOOK OF PEACE PERMANENTLY ETCHED ON HIS FACE.
THE ONLY COMFORT I HAD IN THAT MOMENT WAS KNOWING THAT HE WAS NO LONGER SUFFERING.
BUT HIS BODY WAS NOW AN EMPTY VESSEL. HIS SOUL WOULD NEVER ANIMATE HIS BODY AGAIN. THIS WAS THE LAST TIME I WAS EVER GOING TO PHYSICALLY SEE HIM EVER AGAIN.
HE WASN'T COMING TO MY WEDDING. HE WASN'T GOING TO MEET MY CHILDREN. I WOULD NEVER KNOW WHAT HAPPENED TO HIM WHILE HE WAS IN THE GULAGS.

SEPTEMBER 20, 2011
I'LL ALWAYS REGRET THE FACT THAT I DIDN'T START RECORDING HIS LIFE BEFORE HE GOT SICK. EVEN TODAY, THERE'S STILL SO MUCH I WANT TO ASK HIM.
BUT THAT PRIVILEGE IS NOW GONE FOREVER. AT HIS FUNERAL, I REMEMBER FEELING DEEPLY HURT BECAUSE, EVEN THOUGH I KNEW HIM ALL MY LIFE, I FELT LIKE I WAS JUST STARTING TO UNDERSTAND HIM AND NOW HE WAS GONE FOREVER.
AT FIRST, I HELD ALL OF MY EMOTIONS INSIDE. I WAS TERRIFIED TO FACE THEM.
BUT BY THE TIME I FINALLY CAME HOME, I WAS A WRECK.
THE MOMENT I WAS FINALLY ALONE IS WHEN IT HIT ME. I CRIED LIKE NEVER BEFORE.
MY CHEST ACHED. MY FACE BURNED. MY VOICE WENT DEEP AND THEN SUDDENLY CRACKED. I BECAME WEAK AND FEVERISH. I NEVER CRIED LIKE THAT BEFORE IN MY LIFE.
I HATED EVERY SECOND OF IT.

I WAITED A FEW WEEKS FOR THINGS TO SETTLE BEFORE RESUMING MY RESEARCH. BUT NOW I HAD TO DEPEND ON MY GRANDMOTHER TO FILL IN THE MISSING GAPS FOR ME.
BABUSHKA, I HAVE SOME QUESTIONS FOR YOU REGARDING THE PERIOD WHEN DEDUSHKA WAS IN THE GULAG.
ASK ME YOUR QUESTIONS *BUT--*

--MAKE *SURE* YOU WRITING ABOUT DEDUSHKA'S LOVE FOR *ME!* THAT IS *ONLY* WAY YOUR STORY WILL BE *INTERESTING.*
FOR SOME REASON ALL SHE WANTED TO DO WAS TALK ABOUT HERSELF.

THAT IS *NOT* IMPORTANT FOR THE STORY I'M WRITING. I NEED TO KNOW WHAT HAPPENED WHILE DEDUSHKA WAS IN PRISON.
AND EVERY TIME I TRIED TO DRIVE THE CONVERSATION IN THE DIRECTION THAT I NEEDED IT TO GO...

...SHE IMMEDIATELY FOUND A WAY TO PUT THE SPOTLIGHT BACK ON HER.
NO ONE WHO READ THIS BOOK *CARE* ABOUT WHAT HAPPENING IN PRISON. ALL HE DO IS *WORKING* FOR FIVE YEAR! *VSE!*

WELL I *DO* CARE WHAT HAPPENED TO HIM IN PRISON AND I *NEED* TO KNOW. CAN YOU PLEASE JUST TELL ME *SOMETHING?*
I HAD REACHED MY LIMIT AND SHE KNEW IT.
OKAY. I TELL YOU SOMETHING.

AFTER HE WAS ARRESTED ON THE FRONT LINES, MARX WOKE TO FIND HIMSELF DEEP INSIDE THE CONFINES OF *LEFORTOVO PRISON.*
HE DID NOTHING WRONG. HE WAS AN INNOCENT MAN.
HE HAD NO IDEA WHY HE WAS BROUGHT THERE...
...BUT HE WAS ABOUT TO FIND OUT.
WAKE UP!

MARX MELNIK. SON OF MOSES MELNIK--*ENEMY OF THE STATE.*
WE HAVE REASON TO BELIEVE THAT YOU'RE A *NAZI SPY.*
THAT'S *BULLSHIT!* I'M *JEWISH!*
JEWS WILL DO ANYTHING TO SURVIVE. EXPLAIN THESE LETTERS YOU'VE BEEN PASSING BACK AND FORTH TO YOUR "FRIEND"--ALL WRITTEN IN CODE!
THEY WERE ADDRESSED TO *ELENA SABOTSKIYA,* A CITIZEN OF THE SOVIET UNTION--*NOT A FUCKING NAZI!*
STOP LYING, JEW! YOUR FATHER WAS AN *ENEMY OF THE STATE* AND *YOU* ARE AN *ENEMY OF THE STATE!*

MOTHER RUSSIA DOESN'T TOLERATE TREACHERY.
CONFESS NOW--
--OR YOU WILL BE EXECUTED.
YOUR SILENCE IS PROOF OF YOUR GUILT.
MY FATHER WAS AN INNOCENT MAN!
KRAAAK!

BASHING THAT CHAIR OVER THE INTERROGATOR'S HEAD GOT MARX THROWN INTO A SPECIAL CELL THAT WAS TIGHTLY PACKED WITH OTHER PRISONERS. THEY WERE LIKE PIGS WAITING TO BE BUTCHERED IN A SLAUGHTERHOUSE.
THERE WAS ONE BUCKET MEANT TO BE USED FOR GOING TO THE BATHROOM. IT WAS FILLED TO THE BRIM WITH PISS AND SHIT AND SO THE PRISONERS JUST WENT ON THE FLOOR.
THE ONLY FOOD THAT WAS GIVEN TO THEM WAS SALTED HERRING, WHICH WOULD INCREASE THEIR THIRST FOR WATER.
THEY KNEW THEY WEREN'T GOING TO BE GIVEN WATER BUT ONCE STARVATION KICKED IN, THEY NO LONGER CARED.
THE FRONT LINES WERE HEAVEN COMPARED TO THIS HELL.
RATHER THAN GIVE THE PRISONERS SOMETHING TO DRINK, THE GUARDS DUNKED THEIR HEADS IN WOODEN TUBS FILLED WITH DIRTY, ICE COLD WATER, NEARLY DROWNING THEM.
GET OUT HERE, YOU *PIECE OF SHIT!*
AFTER HOURS OF TORTURE, MARX WAS DRAGGED INTO ANOTHER ROOM WHERE HE WAS EXPECTING TO BE SHOT.

LEAVE THE ROOM. I WILL DEAL WITH THE PRISONER MYSELF.
YES, SIR.
YOU LOOK COLD. WOULD YOU LIKE SOME TEA?
I HAVE SOME WARM CLOTHES FOR YOU IN HERE.
KEEP THEM. THEY ARE YOURS.
WHY ARE YOU BEING SO NICE TO ME?
BECAUSE I KNOW OF YOUR FATHER. HE WAS A SMART MAN.
I READ ABOUT HIM. HE WAS ARRESTED. HE WAS NO SPY-- AND I DON'T BELIEVE YOU ARE, EITHER.
IF YOU'RE GOING TO KILL ME, JUST DO IT ALREADY.
LISTEN TO ME CAREFULLY, SON.
YOU WILL NOT BE EXECUTED.

EAT. YOU MUST BE STARVING AND YOU PROBABLY WON'T BE FED FOR SOME TIME AFTER THIS.
YOU WILL HAVE TO CARRY OUT A FIVE-YEAR PRISON TERM. I'M SORRY, BUT IT'S THE BEST I CAN DO. BUT AT LEAST YOU'LL BE ALIVE.
...THANK YOU.
MARX WASN'T CRYING BECAUSE HIS LIFE WAS SPARED. HE WAS CRYING BECAUSE HE KNEW THAT HIS FATHER WAS WATCHING OVER HIM.
FOR YEARS, MARX WAS TOLD THAT HIS FATHER WAS AN ENEMY OF THE STATE...
...AND NOW, IN HIS DARKEST MOMENT, IT WAS THE PRISON'S WARDEN, OF ALL PEOPLE, WHO SHOWED HIM COMPASSION.
THE NEXT DAY, HE BOARDED A TRAIN AND WAS SENT TO A GULAG IN CHERNOESTOCHINSK, LOCATED SOUTH OF MOSCOW.

IF HE STAY ON FRONT LINE, HE WOULD HAVE *DIED.*
HE SURVIVE *BECAUSE* HE GO TO PRISON.
HE LIVE VERY HARD LIFE.
I UNDERSTOOD WHY MARX NEVER SPOKE ABOUT THE GULAGS AND WHY EVEN MY GRANDMOTHER DIDN'T WANT TO GET INTO IT.
THERE HAD TO BE SHAME IN KNOWING THAT HE SURVIVED THE WAR BECAUSE HE WAS TAKEN PRISONER BY HIS OWN GOVERNMENT.
FOOD WAS EXTREMELY SCARCE. THERE WERE TIMES WHEN MARX WAS STARVING SO BADLY THAT HE ACTUALLY ATE GLUE TO SURVIVE.
THERE WAS NOTHING GLORIOUS ABOUT IT. NOTHING WORTH REMEMBERING.
IT WAS SURVIVAL IN ITS PUREST FORM.

EVERY PRISONER WAS ASSIGNED A NUMBER SO THAT THE GUARDS COULD TELL THEM APART.
ONE LETTER FOLLOWED BY THREE DIGITS.
THAT WAS WHAT DEFINED MARX FOR THE NEXT FIVE YEARS. HE WAS A NUMBER. NOT A PERSON.
FOR FIVE YEARS HE SURVIVED ON PAIKA--A DRIED UP, SOMETIMES EVEN MOLDY, PIECE OF BREAD--AND A RUSTED TIN MUG FILLED WITH WATER. HE WAS FED JUST ENOUGH TO SURVIVE.
PART OF SURVIVING THE GULAGS WAS LEARNING HOW TO BARTER WITH THE OTHER PRISONERS.
I'LL TRADE YOU MY PAIKA FOR YOUR JACKET.
GLADLY.
THE CONDITIONS WERE VERY HARSH. MARX WAS ALWAYS EITHER COLD OR STARVING.
SO COLD.
BUT HE ALSO TRIED TO RETAIN SOME SENSE OF HIS OWN MORAL COMPASS.
I CAN BARELY FEEL ANYTHING.
SOMETIMES KNOWING THAT HE WAS STILL HUMAN WAS WORTH MORE THAN EATING OR STAYING WARM.
BLESS YOUR HEART, BOY.

MY GRANDMOTHER LATER TOLD ME THAT MARX OFTEN KEPT IN TOUCH WITH ONE OF THE PEOPLE HE SURVIVED THE GULAGS WITH AND THAT THIS MAN WAS STILL ALIVE AND LIVING IN BERLIN, GERMANY.
HIS NAME WAS SASHA CHUSMEAR AND HE WAS VERY ILL AND GOING BLIND.
MARX'S DEATH TAUGHT ME TO SEIZE WHATEVER INFORMATION I COULD GET WHILE IT WAS STILL AVAILABLE AND SO I FELT THIS HUGE SENSE OF URGENCY TO MEET WITH SASHA IMMEDIATELY BEFORE THE OPPORTUNITY WOULD BE LOST FOREVER.
COME IN!
I WAS SO NERVOUS THAT I WOULDN'T MAKE IT TO HIM IN TIME AND THAT HE WOULD BE TOO SICK TO TALK TO ME.
I'M MARX MELNIK'S GRANDSON. I WAS-
YES, YES, I KNOW WHO YOU ARE. HAVE A SEAT.
SASHA REMINDED ME A LOT OF MARX. THERE WAS SOMETHING IN HIS DEMEANOR THAT WAS ALMOST IDENTICAL.
FOR THE FIRST TIME IN MY LIFE, I FINALLY UNDERSTOOD HOW OUTSIDERS PERCEIVED MY GRANDFATHER. HE WASN'T THE MOST OUTGOING PERSON. IN FACT, HE COULD BE A REAL ASSHOLE.
SASHA WAS NINETY YEARS OLD WHEN I MET HIM. HE WAS TWO YEARS OLDER THAN MARX AND HIS WIFE HAD DIED MANY YEARS BEFORE. THEY MET IN A GULAG.
ACK! ACK! AGGKKKR!
CAN YOU TELL ME ABOUT THE GULAG?
I WROTE A BOOK ABOUT IT. YOU SHOULD READ IT.
I DON'T READ RUSSIAN.
BUT YOU SPEAK IT? WHAT THE HELL IS THIS WORLD COMING TO?
VERY WELL. I'LL TELL YOU ABOUT YOUR GRANDFATHER.

I MET MARX IN 1943. HE WAS AMONG A GROUP OF PRISONERS THAT WERE TRANSFERRED FROM A GULAG IN *CHERNOISTOCHINSK* TO *NEZNI TAGIL.*
THE PRISONERS WERE FORCED TO WALK TO *NEZNI TAGIL.* THE JOURNEY WAS CALLED AN *ETAP.*
MANY OF THEM DIED ALONG THE WAY.
WHENEVER A NEW PRISONER WOULD COME, THEY WERE IMMEDIATELY WELCOMED. THERE WAS A LOT OF WORK TO DO AND WE WERE ALWAYS UNDERMANNED.
YOUR GRANDFATHER AND I WERE BOTH ENGINEERS BY TRADE. WE BUILT AN ENTIRE AIRPORT WHILE WE WERE IN THE GULAG.
WE SPENT A YEAR TOGETHER BEFORE HE WAS SENT ON ANOTHER ETAP. AFTER THE WAR ENDED, WE FOUND EACH OTHER AND REMAINED AS FRIENDS.

YOUR GRANDFATHER WAS A HARD WORKER. WE GOT ALONG VERY WELL.
SO WHY ARE YOU HERE?
HEH. FOR A **DAMN** STUPID REASON.
I WAS A BOMBER AND GIVEN SPECIFIC COORDINATES TO HIT.
BY THE TIME I RETURNED TO BASE, I DISCOVERED THAT THE SOVIETS HAD LIBERATED THE STRONGHOLD THAT I HAD JUST BOMBED.
I WAS RESPONSIBLE FOR KILLING OUR OWN SOLDIERS.
THE FUNNY THING IS THAT I'VE NEVER HIT A TARGET SO ACCURATELY IN MY LIFE.
I WAS SLAPPED WITH A TEN-YEAR PRISON TERM.
SO WHAT'S YOUR STORY, MARX?
MY FATHER IS AN ENEMY OF THE STATE. I WAS ARRESTED ON SUSPICION OF BEING A JEW WHO CONSPIRED WITH THE NAZIS. THEY GAVE ME ***FIVE YEARS.***
THAT'S IT? JUST ***FIVE YEARS?!*** LUCKY BASTARD*!*

WE USUALLY DIDN'T SPEAK MUCH. IT WAS ALWAYS BETTER TO KEEP TO YOURSELF.
WHY?
BECAUSE ONE DAY WE HEARD GUNSHOTS COMING FROM OUTSIDE OUR SHOP. A RUMOR BEGAN TO SPREAD THAT THE ROOM NEXT TO US WAS FULL OF PRISONERS THAT HAD LOTS OF GREAT THOUGHTS ABOUT CAPITALISM.
WE NEVER SAW ANY BODIES BUT WE LATER NOTICED DRIED BLOOD STAINS ON THE FLOORS AND WALLS. THE GUARDS ENJOYED INSTILLING FEAR INTO THE PRISONERS BY KILLING ANYONE THAT GAVE THEM THE SLIGHTEST REASON.
WHETHER WHAT HAPPENED WAS TRUE OR NOT, IT WASN'T WORTH IT TO BE GUNNED DOWN FOR HAVING A LOOSE TONGUE.
IT WAS A MESSAGE WELL RECEIVED.

WE WERE LUCKY. WE WEREN'T SENTENCED TO HARD LABOR THOUGH. NOW, THAT WAS A DEATH SENTENCE.
PRISONERS THAT WORKED OUTSIDE ALL DAY WERE OFTEN ATTACKED BY MOSQUITOES. CONSIDERING HOW LITTLE FOOD AND WATER WE WERE GIVEN, EVEN *MOSQUITOES* COULD *KILL* YOU.
SO MANY PEOPLE DIED.
AKKKG!
I'M SORRY BUT I NEED TO *AKKKG!* LIE DOWN.
LIKE MARX, SASHA HAD BEEN THROUGH HELL AND BACK. I GOT ALL I COULD FROM HIM...

...BUT I STILL HAD QUESTIONS.
AS SOON AS I RETURNED FROM BERLIN, THE FIRST PLACE I WENT WAS MARX'S STUDY.
YEARS AGO, I REMEMBER HIM SHOWING ME A PORTRAIT THAT SOMEONE HAD DRAWN OF HIM WHILE HE WAS IN THE GULAG.
HE KEPT IT SOMEWHERE IN HIS DESK BUT I COULDN'T FIND IT.
I SPENT A HALF HOUR DIGGING AROUND TRYING TO FIND IT. MARX WAS EXTREMELY ORGANIZED AND, HAD HE BEEN AROUND, HE WOULD HAVE EASILY BEEN ABLE TO SHOW ME WHERE EVERYTHING WAS.
WHERE THE FUCK IS IT?!!!
BUT HE WASN'T AND THAT FRUSTRATED ME MORE THAN NOT BEING ABLE TO FIND WHAT I WAS LOOKING FOR.
OH SHIT!
I HAD FOUND WHAT I WAS LOOKING FOR.

SORAV, RUSSIA
MAY 9TH, 1945
SIT STILL, MARX. I'M NOT DONE YET.
I'M DYING FOR A CIGARETTE, KIRILLOV.
ATTENTION, ATTENTION! FOR THOSE OF YOU JUST TUNING IN, ON THIS DAY, MAY 9TH OF 1945, THE NAZI PARTY HAS SURRENDERED TO RUSSIA. THE WAR IS WON!
THERE. IT'S FINISHED!
WHAT DO YOU THINK, MARX?
IT LOOKS NOTHING LIKE ME.
SO THE WAR'S OVER NOW. WHO GIVES A SHIT? WE'RE STILL PRISONERS.
NOT FOR LONG. NOW THAT THE WAR IS OVER, STALIN HAS NO REASON TO KEEP SO MANY PEOPLE IN PRISON.
THERE ARE RUMORS THAT WE'LL ALL BE LET OUT SOON.
I'M GOING TO LEAVE THIS PLACE, MOVE TO FRANCE, AND BECOME A FAMOUS ARTIST!
I'LL BELIEVE IT WHEN I SEE IT.
SHH! BOTH OF YOU! WE'RE TRYING TO LISTEN TO THE RADIO.

WEEKS PASSED AND IT TURNED OUT THAT KIRILLOV WAS RIGHT.
I'M A FREE MAN! I CAN FINALLY LEAVE THIS PLACE!
LOOKS LIKE YOU PROVED ME WRONG.
I EXPECT TO SEE YOU ON THE OTHER SIDE SOON AS WELL, MY FRIEND.
AKKKKG! AKKKKKG!
I--I'M FINE.
KEEP THE FAITH, ***MARX MOSEIVICH.***

A FEW DAYS LATER, KIRILLOV DIED.
MARX HAD NO FAITH LEFT TO KEEP. OPTIMISM WAS THE FOOL'S WAY OF THINKING.
HE WAS NOW CONVINCED THAT HE WOULD NEVER SEE THE OUTSIDE OF THE GULAGS.

A YEAR AFTER THE WAR ENDED, MARX WAS SENT ON A FINAL ETAP TO VERKHOYANSK.
HE WASN'T COUNTING ON ANY LUCK TO COME HIS WAY.
OFF THE TRAIN!
MARX MOSEIVICH!

IT WAS ELENA SABOTSKIYA. AFTER THE WAR ENDED, SHE TRACKED MARX DOWN.
I'M SO GLAD YOU'RE ALIVE! WE DON'T HAVE MUCH TIME. I HAVE A HOME IN ALEXANDROV. WHEN THEY LET YOU OUT, COME FIND ME THERE.
WHAT ARE YOU DOING HERE, ELENA? GO HOME.
WHAT DO YOU MEAN?
I MEAN YOU SHOULDN'T BE HERE. FORGET THAT I EXIST.
THE GOVERNMENT IS GIVING AMNESTY TO PRISONERS NOW THAT THE WAR IS OVER. WHAT ARE YOU GOING TO DO IF YOUR SENTENCE IS REDUCED?
I'LL WORRY ABOUT THAT WHEN THE TIME COMES.
FIND ME! I'LL TAKE CARE OF YOU.

I OFTEN WONDERED WHAT KEPT MARX GOING. IT CERTAINLY WASN'T THE HOPE THAT ONE DAY HE WOULD BE FREE FROM PRISON.
OR WAS IT?
MAYBE IT WAS THE THOUGHT OF THE LOVE HIS PARENTS HAD FOR EACH OTHER THAT KEPT HIM ALIVE. THAT, AND KNOWING WHAT HIS FATHER WENT THROUGH TO KEEP HIM ALIVE.
HE OWED IT TO THEM TO SURVIVE AND TO BE HAPPY EVEN THOUGH HE WAS MISERABLE. BUT HE DIDN'T KNOW LOVE AND I DOUBT HE BELIEVED IT EXISTED WITHIN THE WALLS OF THE GULAGS.
ALL HE KNEW WAS THAT HE HAD TO KEEP LIVING UNTIL HIS BODY FINALLY GAVE UP ON HIM.
THE TRUTH IS THAT I DON'T KNOW WHAT HE WAS THINKING AND FEELING AFTER ALL THOSE YEARS IN PRISON.
BUT I BELIEVE WITH ALL MY HEART THAT THERE WAS SOME SMALL PART OF HIM THAT HELD ONTO THE HOPE THAT LIFE COULD GET BETTER...

...AND THAT HE WOULD ONE DAY FIND SOMEONE THAT HE LOVED AS MUCH AS MOSES LOVED ELIZABETH.
BABUSHKA?
CAN YOU TELL ME HOW YOU MET HIM?

CHAPTER 6:

LABOR OF LOVE

Onrie Kompan
WRITER

Nick Bell
ARTIST

Ben Dimagmaliw
COLORIST

Ed Dukeshire
LETTERER

JM DeMatteis
EDITOR

YOU STILL COOKING?! IT TAKE YOU ***THIRTY MINUTES*** TO MAKE DINNER!

YOU ARE LIKE BLOOD SUCKING MONKEY, MARX! ***I CAN'T STAND YOU ANYMORE!***

BE QUIET. YOU TALKING TOO MUCH.

YOU WORK ME LIKE SLAVE!

MARX. MY POOR MARX.
ON THE DAY THAT MARX PASSED AWAY THOUGH, I NEVER SAW MY GRANDMOTHER FLARE UP WITH SUCH EMOTION.
MY HUSBAND IS DEAD! MY HUSBAND IS DEAD!
AS IF ALL THE FIGHTING AND BICKERING NEVER EVEN MATTERED. THAT WASN'T THE BIG PICTURE OR THE PURPOSE OF THE LIFE THEY SHARED TOGETHER.
THE MOMENT MARX DIED IS WHEN I REALIZED HOW IMPORTANT THEIR MARRIAGE WAS TO THEM. THEY DEFINED EACH OTHER.
AT HIS FUNERAL, SHE WALKED UP TO HIS CASKET AND STARTED TALKING TO HIM AS IF HE WERE STILL ALIVE.
REST NOW, MARACHKA. EVERYTHING OKAY.
GROWING UP, I SOMETIMES WONDERED WHY THEY DIDN'T JUST GET A DIVORCE.
AFTER THE FUNERAL, WE ALL THOUGHT SHE WOULD BE OKAY.
BUT AS THE YEARS PASSED, SHE GREW SADDER.
MARACHKA, I MISS YOU. TELL ME YOU LOVE ME. I ALWAYS THINK OF YOU.
SHE STILL TALKS TO HIM EVERY TIME SHE COMES TO HIS GRAVE. AS IF HE WERE STILL ALIVE TO HEAR HER.

IN ORDER FOR ME TO PUT CLOSURE TO HIS LIFE AND TO HIS STORY, I NEEDED TO UNDERSTAND THE LOVE MARX HAD FOR HIS WIFE.
WHERE DID IT COME FROM?

ANYA.
SHE OFTEN TELLS ME THAT MARX'S ABSENCE WEIGHS SO HEAVILY ON HER SOUL THAT IT FEELS LIKE A HUGE ANVIL WAS DROPPED ON HER CHEST.

THIS IS HOW MY GRANDMOTHER HAS BEEN LIVING HER LIFE EVER SINCE MARX PASSED AWAY.

AT FIRST, SHE DID WHATEVER SHE COULD TO REMOVE THAT DEAD WEIGHT ON HER CHEST.
SOMEONE TOLD HER THAT NO ONE SHOULD WEAR THE SHOES OF A LOVED ONE WHO HAS PASSED AND SO SHE CUT UP ALL OF MARX'S SHOES AND THREW THEM IN THE TRASH.

THEN SHE TRIED TO GET ME TO WEAR HIS CLOTHES.
BABUSHKA, THIS DOESN'T FIT ME.
WHAT YOU TALKING ABOUT? IS LOOK ***GREAT*** ON YOU!

IF NOT FOR SURGEONS, HE STILL BE ALIVE TODAY.

EVENTUALLY, SHE STOPPED TRYING TO REMOVE THE DEAD WEIGHT AND SHE FORCED HERSELF TO LIVE WITH IT.

SHE CONSTANTLY RECALLS MARX'S FINAL DAYS AS IF I HADN'T BEEN AROUND WHEN IT HAPPENED.
BUT I *WAS* THERE. I KNOW WHAT HAPPENED. STILL I SIT THERE IN SILENCE AS SHE TELLS HER STORY AND I NEVER HAVE ANY IDEA WHAT I'M SUPPOSED TO SAY AFTERWARDS.

THINGS WERE SO MUCH EASIER WHEN MARX WAS AROUND. NOW THERE IS ONLY ONE WAY FOR ME TO CHEER HER UP.
BABUSHKA, WHY DON'T YOU TELL ME HOW YOU MET DEDUSHKA?
YOU ALREADY KNOW THIS STORY. WHY YOU WANT ME TO TELL YOU AGAIN?
BECAUSE IT ALWAYS PUTS A SMILE ON YOUR FACE.
YOU ARE SWEET BOY. OKAY, I TELL YOU HOW WE MEET.

SAROV, RUSSIA
DECEMBER 26, 1947
IT ALL BEGIN IN A RUSSIA WHEN MARX WAS RELEASE FROM GULAG TWO YEAR AFTER WAR END.
HE HAVE NOWHERE TO GO. HIS RELATIVES NOT WANT HIM BECAUSE HE WAS ENEMY OF STATE.
HIS DOCUMENTS SAY HE NOT ALLOWED TO GO TO BIG CITY AND SO HE CAN'T GO TO NINA KLUEVA IN MOSCOW. HE WAS ALONE AND SO HE GO TO ALEXANDROV WHERE ELENA SABOTSKIYA WAITING FOR HIM.

LIFE OUTSIDE OF GULAG WAS NO EASY THAN LIFE INSIDE. PEOPLE STILL VERY POOR AND HUNGRY.

AT LEAST IN PRISON, THEY GIVE EVERYONE BREAD AND WATER.
MARX HAD TO TAKE CARE OF HIMSELF. ANY WAY HE CAN.

HE CAME!
OH MARX! I AM SO GLAD YOU'RE HERE!
I HAD NOWHERE ELSE TO GO.

HE NOT LOVE ELENA. BUT SHE OFFER BED TO SLEEP IN. SOON SHE SAY TO HIM.
I'M PREGNANT.

I WANT TO KEEP THE BABY. YOU DON'T NEED TO HELP ME TAKE CARE OF IT.
THIS IS MY CHILD, TOO. WE WILL GET MARRIED AND HE WILL HAVE MY NAME.

I HAVE AN UNCLE IN KURSK. HE WILL GET ME WORK. I WILL PROVIDE FOR BOTH OF YOU.
I DON'T WANT TO LIVE THERE. THIS IS MY HOME. I FINISHED MY EDUCATION AND I PLAN TO TEACH HERE. NOT IN KURSK.
FINE. I'LL GO WORK AND COME HOME ON THE WEEKENDS.

MARX VERY RESPONSIBLE MAN. WHENEVER HE MAKE PROMISE, HE *ALWAYS* KEEP IT. FOR ELENA, HE MAKE PROMISE, EVEN THOUGH SHE NOT MAKE HIM HAPPY.

YOU'RE LOOKING GOOD, MY BOY! WHAT CAN I DO FOR YOU?
I'M LOOKING FOR WORK, UNCLE.
I'M NOT SURE I CAN HELP YOU.

I'M NOT ASKING FOR HELP. WHATEVER IT IS, I CAN DO IT BETTER THAN ANYONE ELSE.
OKAY, OKAY. LET ME SEE WHAT I CAN DO.

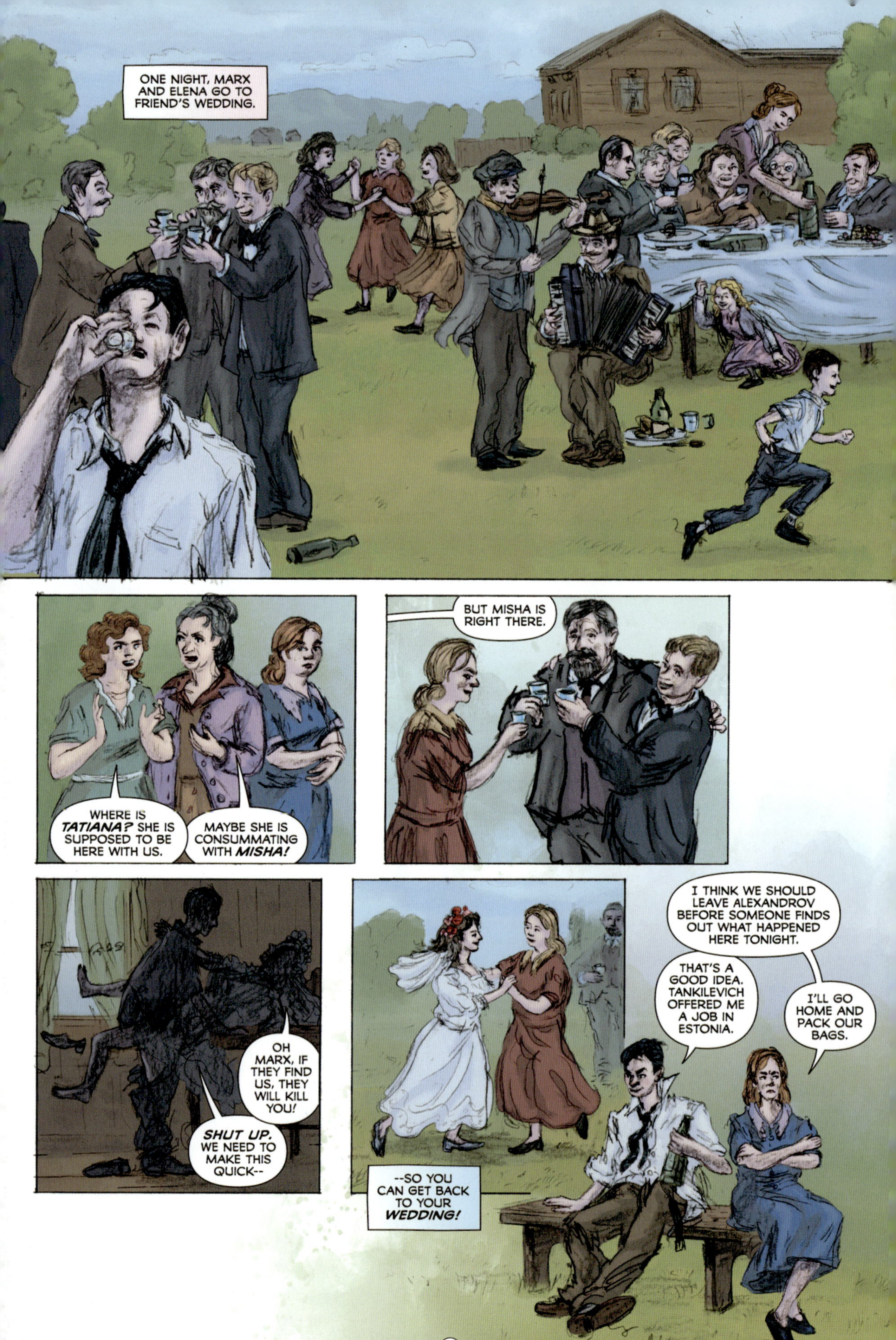

ONE NIGHT, MARX AND ELENA GO TO FRIEND'S WEDDING.

MARX NOT BAD MAN. HE LOVE HIS SON VERY MUCH. HE JUST WAS NO GOOD AT SHOWING IT.

BECAUSE HIS LIFE WAS EMPTY.

BABUSHKA, WHERE WERE YOU WHILE ALL THIS WAS HAPPENING?

I WAS HAPPILY MARRIED TO SOMEBODY ELSE.

SO WHAT IS THIS SURPRISE YOU HAVE FOR ME IN ESTONIA, YASHA? YOU KNOW I'LL NEVER CALL THAT PLACE MY HOME.

SOMETHING TELLS ME YOU'RE GOING TO LIKE IT THERE.

HERE WE ARE.

SO WHAT DO YOU THINK?
WHO CARES WHAT I THINK? IT'S NOT LIKE IT'S OURS.

IT IS NOW. WE OWN IT.

YASHA! YOU CAN'T BE SERIOUS!

IT'S BEAUTIFUL! I LOVE IT!
I WANT YOU TO HAVE EVERYTHING YOU WANT.
I ***DO*** HAVE EVERYTHING I WANT! I AM THE ***LUCKIEST*** WOMAN IN THE SOVIET UNION!

BUT ELENA WAS *MOST* MISERABLE.
SHHH SHHH SHHH! EVERYTHING IS OKAY, SASHINKA. STOP CRYING. PAPA IS COMING!

WHERE ARE *YOU* GOING?
WORK.
BUT IT'S SATURDAY.

SO WHAT?

WE NEED THE MONEY.

HOW COULD HE BE SO COLD TO ELENA?
IT'S NOT THAT HE COLD TO HER, ONRISHINKA. THIS WAS THE TIME. EVERYONE HAVE TO WORK HARD TO LIVE. LIFE AFTER WAR WAS VERY DIFFICULT.

MARX FEEL VERY LOST. EVEN THOUGH HE HAVE GOOD JOB, HE WAS NOT HAPPY BECAUSE HE SETTLE WITH SOMEONE HE NOT LOVE.
ONE NIGHT, HE GO OUT TO DINNER WITH HIS BOSS AND THEN THEY DECIDE TO GO FOR WALK.
SO WHERE ARE WE GOING?
I HONESTLY HAVE NO IDEA.

I LOVE NIGHT SKIES!
BIG FUCKING SURPRISE.
WHAT WAS THAT?
YES-- *YES!* SO DO I.
OH! WE'RE IN *YASHA'S* NEIGHBORHOOD. LET'S VISIT HIM.

I'D RATHER NOT. WE DON'T KNOW EACH OTHER THAT WELL.
NONSENSE! HIS WIFE INSISTED THAT I COME VISIT THEM AT SOME POINT. I'VE BEEN MEANING TO BUT I'VE BEEN SO BUSY AT WORK.

THIS BUILDING IS A REAL SHITHOLE.
WHAT WAS THAT?
I DIDN'T SAY ANYTHING. KEEP WALKING.
BOZHE MOI.

JUST WAIT UNTIL YOU MEET HIS WIFE. SHE IS ABSOLUTELY CHARMING.
WHO IS IT?

HELLO, ANYA! THIS IS *MARX MOSEIVICH MELNIK*. SAY HELLO TO ANYA, MARX.
MARX?
OH! *ABRAHAM GREGORIVICH!* SO NICE TO SEE YOU! WHO IS THIS YOU HAVE WITH YOU?
WHEN MARX FIRST LOOK AT ME, HE FREEZE!
HE TELL ME HIS HEART WAS BEATING FASTER. HIS HANDS WERE COLD.
HE WAS IN LOVE WITH ME *FIRST SIGHT.*

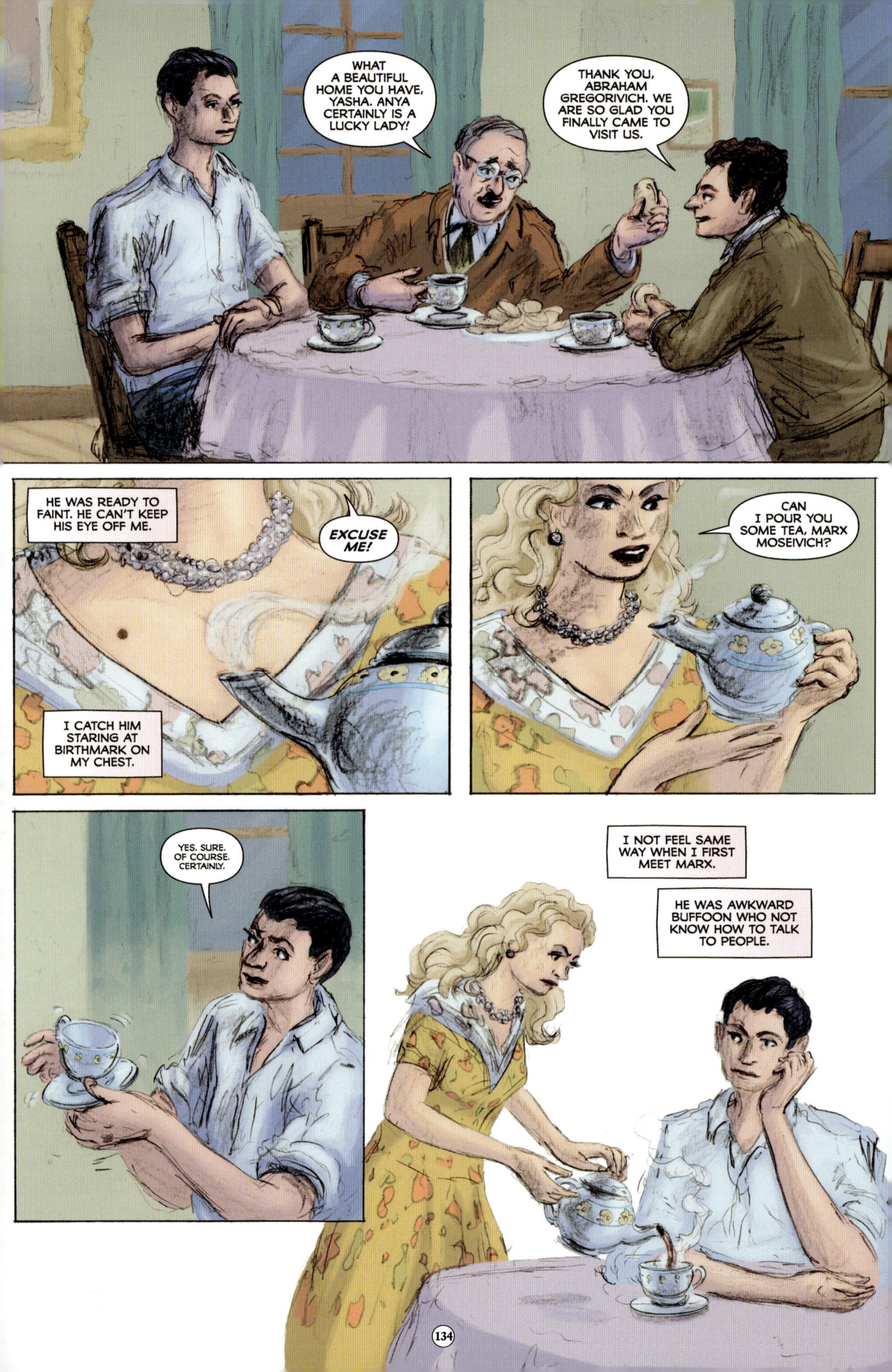

WHAT A BEAUTIFUL HOME YOU HAVE, YASHA. ANYA CERTAINLY IS A LUCKY LADY!

THANK YOU, ABRAHAM GREGORIVICH. WE ARE SO GLAD YOU FINALLY CAME TO VISIT US.

YES. SURE. OF COURSE. CERTAINLY.

I NOT FEEL SAME WAY WHEN I FIRST MEET MARX.

HE WAS AWKWARD BUFFOON WHO NOT KNOW HOW TO TALK TO PEOPLE.

I REALLY DIDN'T LIKE *MARX MOSEIVICH.* HE WAS SO AWKWARD. I THINK HE MIGHT HAVE BRAIN DAMAGE.
FAR FROM IT. THE MAN IS A GENIUS ACCORDING TO TANKELEVICH. HE WON'T SHUT UP ABOUT HIM.

I'M SURE TANKELEVICH SAYS JUST AS MUCH ABOUT *YOU* TO MARX.

MARX SEEMED SMITTEN WITH YOU THOUGH.
EH. HE'S STILL AN IDIOT.

WHERE WERE YOU? IT'S NEARLY MIDNIGHT.

WORKING.
WHY ARE YOU SMILING LIKE AN IDIOT?
IT'S NOTHING. GOOD NIGHT.

MARX COULDN'T SLEEP. ALL HE COULD THINK OF WAS ME. HE HAD TO FIND WAY TO BE WITH *ME.*

HE THEN COME UP WITH VERY *STUPID* IDEA.

SO, HOW ABOUT WE GO TO A CAFÉ TONIGHT AFTER WORK?
I DON'T KNOW. ANYA EXPECTS ME HOME EVERY NIGHT BY SEVEN.

ALL MARRIED WOMEN EVER DO IS MAKE DEMANDS ON US, RIGHT? HOW ABOUT I SET YOU UP WITH...

MARINA!

NO.

NADEZDHA!

NO.

SVETLANA!

NO, NO, AND NO!

I HAVE A BEAUTIFUL WIFE AT HOME. WHY WOULD I CHEAT ON HER?

SHIT.

THEN HE START CALLING ME EVERY DAY.
MARX, STOP CALLING ME.
I HAVEN'T SLEPT IN DAYS. YOU'RE ALL I THINK ABOUT.
FIND A NEW HOBBY. I TOLD YOU ALREADY--I'M MARRIED.
I DON'T CARE. I HAVE TO SEE YOU. COME HAVE COFFEE WITH ME. JUST FOR AN HOUR. I NEED TO SEE YOU!
FINE. TOMORROW NIGHT.
AND DON'T BE LATE.

I LIKE ALL THE ATTENTION MARX GAVE ME.
BUT I LIKE EVEN MORE THAT HE WAS SO INTELLIGENT. SO HANDSOME.
HE WAS DIFFERENT PERSON WITH ME. NOT COLD LIKE WITH OTHERS. I SAW GOOD MAN IN HIM.
SOMEONE WHO UNDERSTAND VALUE OF LIFE.
ANYA, I'M HOME.
HELLO?
I THOUGHT I HAD EVERYTHING I WANTED WITH YASHA. BUT MARX'S LOVE FOR ME MADE ME REALIZE I DIDN'T.
I FELT VERY BAD FOR ELENA. SHE WAS GOOD WOMAN. SHE WAS JUST VICTIM OF MARX'S NEGLECT.

MARX MOSEIVICH! WHERE ARE YOU HIDING YOU SONNAVA BITCH!

SHE IS LEAVING ME! YOU STOLE HER FROM ME!

I'M SORRY, YASHA. I DIDN'T MEAN TO HURT YOU.

YOU ARROGANT SELF-CENTERED PIECE OF SHIT!
I'LL KILL YOU FOR THIS!
STOP IT, YASHA! YOU'RE MAKING A FOOL OF YOURSELF!

YOUR RUINED MY LIFE!

I WAS HOPING THAT ONE DAY YOU WOULD WAKE UP AND BE IN LOVE WITH ME-- BUT NOW I SEE YOU FINALLY FOUND YOUR OTHER HALF.

I'M SO STUPID.

NO, YOU'RE NOT. YOU'RE ONE OF THE SMARTEST AND KINDEST PEOPLE I'VE EVER KNOWN.

I'M STILL GOING TO BE HERE FOR YOU AND SASHA. I WILL ALWAYS SUPPORT YOU.

MARX, I'M PREGNANT AGAIN. IT'S YOURS.

I PROMISE I WILL SUPPORT ALL OF YOU.

MARX WAS MAN OF HIS WORD. HE ALWAYS TAKING CARE OF HIS CHILDREN FROM FIRST MARRIAGE.

BUT ELENA NEVER REMARRIED AFTER MARX LEAVE HER.

DIDN'T YOU HAVE ANY GUILT, BABUSHKA?
OF COURSE I HAVE GUILT! HOW I NOT HAVE GUILT?
WHAT DID WE GET OURSELVES INTO?
WHAT DO YOU MEAN?

WHAT KIND OF PEOPLE ARE WE?
GO BACK TO ELENA, MARX. YOU HAVE A CHILD WITH HER AND SHE'S PREGNANT. WHAT WE'RE DOING ISN'T RIGHT.

SO NOW YOU WANT ME OUT OF YOUR LIFE?
IT'S NOT THAT SIMPLE.
WHEN I WAS TEN, MY MOTHER *DIED* DURING *CHILDBIRTH!*
WHEN I WAS FOURTEEN, MY *FATHER* WAS *MURDERED!*

I'M *DONE* LOSING THE PEOPLE I LOVE FROM MY LIFE!
YOU CAN LEAVE ME IF YOU WANT BUT I'M *NOT LETTING YOU GO.*

I LOVE YOU.

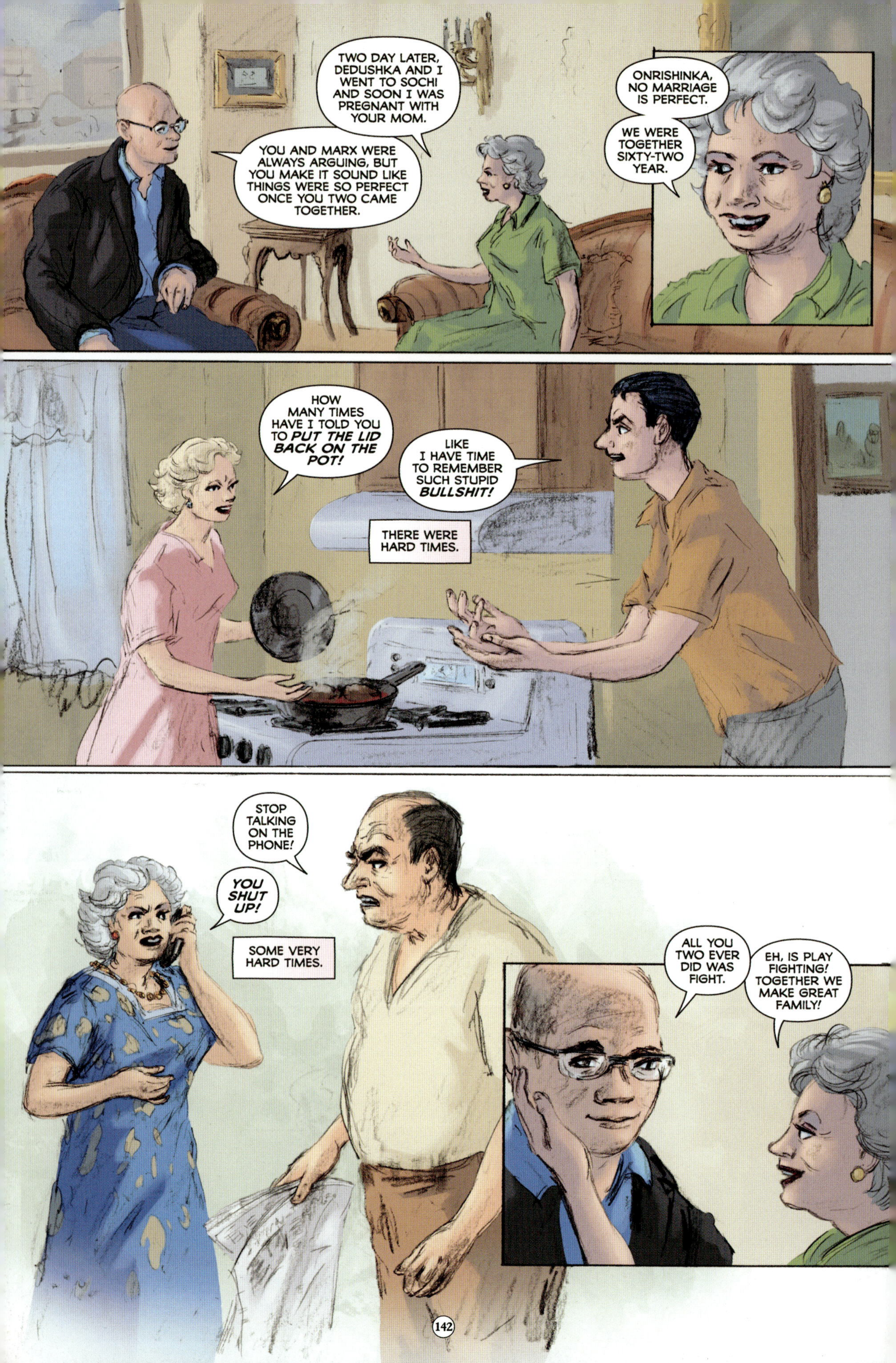
YOU AND MARX WERE ALWAYS ARGUING, BUT YOU MAKE IT SOUND LIKE THINGS WERE SO PERFECT ONCE YOU TWO CAME TOGETHER.
TWO DAY LATER, DEDUSHKA AND I WENT TO SOCHI AND SOON I WAS PREGNANT WITH YOUR MOM.
ONRISHINKA, NO MARRIAGE IS PERFECT.
WE WERE TOGETHER SIXTY-TWO YEAR.
HOW MANY TIMES HAVE I TOLD YOU TO PUT THE LID BACK ON THE POT!
LIKE I HAVE TIME TO REMEMBER SUCH STUPID BULLSHIT!
THERE WERE HARD TIMES.
STOP TALKING ON THE PHONE!
YOU SHUT UP!
SOME VERY HARD TIMES.
ALL YOU TWO EVER DID WAS FIGHT.
EH, IS PLAY FIGHTING! TOGETHER WE MAKE GREAT FAMILY!

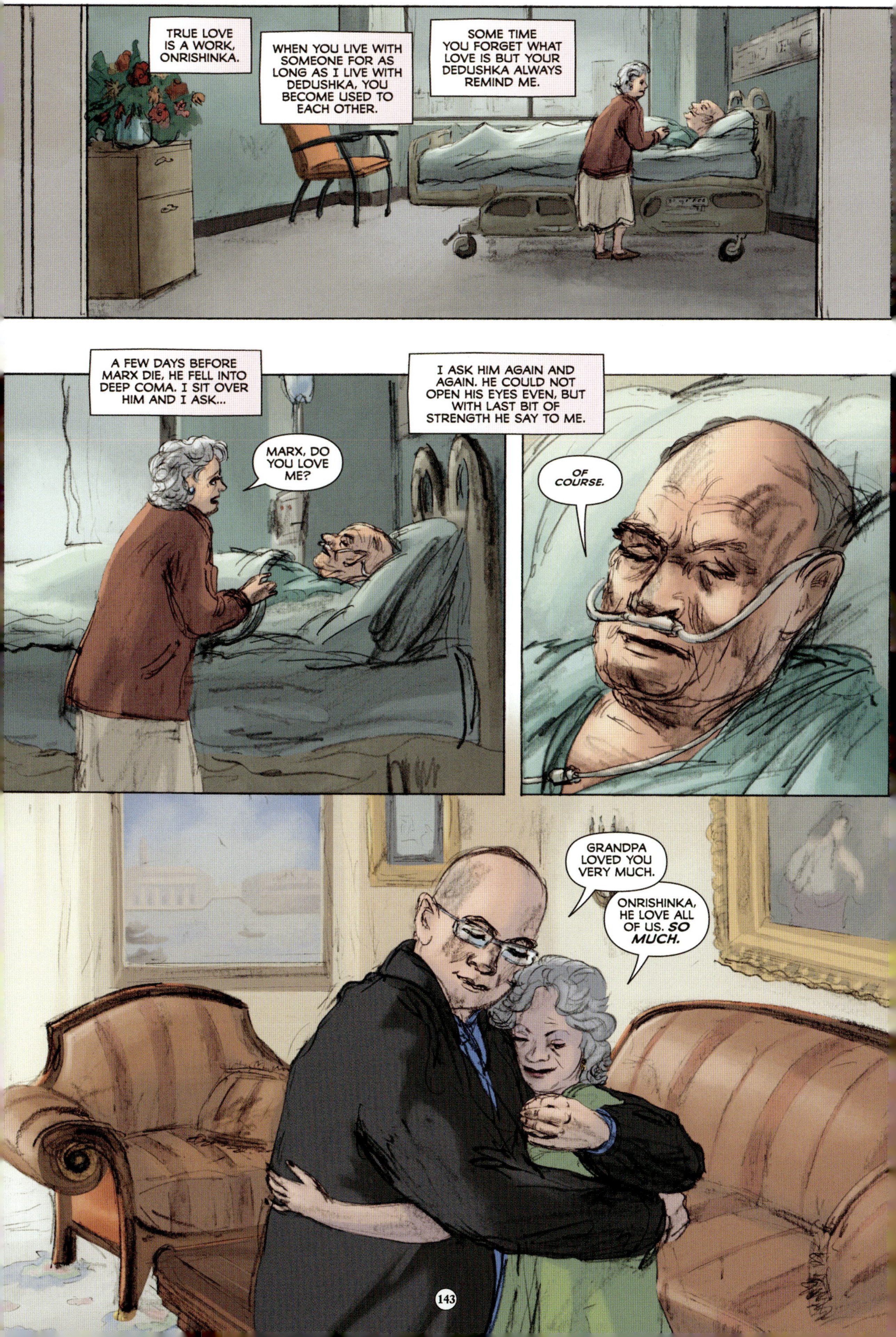

A FEW DAYS BEFORE MARX DIE, HE FELL INTO DEEP COMA. I SIT OVER HIM AND I ASK...

MARX, DO YOU LOVE ME?

I ASK HIM AGAIN AND AGAIN. HE COULD NOT OPEN HIS EYES EVEN, BUT WITH LAST BIT OF STRENGTH HE SAY TO ME.

OF COURSE.

GRANDPA LOVED YOU VERY MUCH.

ONRISHINKA, HE LOVE ALL OF US. ***SO MUCH.***

JUNE 12, 2012.
BEFORE HE DIED, MARX USED TO TELL ME THAT ALL HE WANTED WAS TO SEE ME GET MARRIED AND HAVE CHILDREN.
HE DIED FIVE DAYS BEFORE MY WEDDING. ONE MONTH LATER, MY WIFE WAS PREGNANT WITH OUR SON.
WE NAMED HIM AFTER MARX.
MARX MAY NOT HAVE LIVED TO SEE MY CHILDREN, BUT THEY WILL KNOW HIM. THEY WILL KNOW OF EVERYTHING HE SACRIFICED. THANKS TO HIM THEY WILL NEVER KNOW...
...A LIFE OF NEGLECT.
THE END.